# Human Factor Decay and the Failure of Regulatory Responses to Unethical Business Practices

## EILEEN GRIFFIN AND SENYO ADJIBOLOSOO

outskirtspress
DENVER, COLORADO

Human Factor Decay and the Failure of Regulatory Responses to Unethical Business Practices
All Rights Reserved.
Copyright © 2012 Eileen Griffin and Senyo Adjibolosoo
v2.0

Outskirts Press, Inc.
http://www.outskirtspress.com

ISBN: 978-1-4327-9469-9

Outskirts Press and the "OP" logo are trademarks belonging to Outskirts Press, Inc.

# Contents

# CHAPTER 1

# Introduction

WITH THE END of World War I and the prosperity that followed, the securities industry saw a large increase in the number of investors participating in the stock market. During the 1920s, approximately 20 million people became shareholders, expecting the amassing of more wealth with little or no consideration of the risk of potential loss. But of the $50 billion in securities that was amassed during this time, approximately half disappeared during the stock market crash of 1929 (www.sec.gov/about retrieved 2/23/2010). As a result of the crash and the significant loss of confidence investors now had in the stock market, Congress decided it was time to play a role. With the Securities Act of 1933 and the Securities and Exchange Act of 1934, initial legislation was activated and the Securities and Exchange Commission (SEC) was born. With the securities-related law, Congress stepped into the industry and since then has never taken a step back.

This book begins with a review of the history of legislation enacted to control the brokerage business in the United States. The historical perspective establishes a trend of legislators creating laws, establishing bureaucracies and multiple layers of oversight that have been largely useless and definitely costly. There are significant costs tied to the maintenance of a system that simply accepts and works with the understanding that the players in the industry pursue corrupted, greedy, and unethical practices. Rather than making the effort to correct the problems that face the system by improving the attitudinal and behavioral practices of industry players, government officials currently provide ineffective regulatory remedies to correct the system. Congress has created a number of laws with such burdensome requirements that some brokerage firms have simply had to shut their doors in the face of escalating costs to comply with the demands of the regulators.

At FINRA conferences, complaints are often voiced by the smaller firms that they are drowning in regulations and are barely able to remain profitable with the paperwork and compliance requirements. Firms are expected to respond to auditors regardless of other needs of the staff involved in running the operations. Business can nearly cease during an audit, resulting in a loss of productivity. In addition to costs associated with compliance, firms are burdened with ever-increasing expenses related to Errors and Omissions coverage and legal costs as more consumers are encouraged to file complaints. The media and the government have unfairly made the brokerage industry into the scapegoat for all that has impacted our economy. While there is certainly some responsibility here, this industry is already heavily regulated, and additional regulations will not solve any problems.

Particularly in the last few years, companies that had previously been considered stalwart in corporate society have been exposed, and unethical practices have led to their downfall. This is in spite of several existing laws and systems designed expressly to ensure that business is run fairly and ethically. Regardless of the efforts that federal and state governments have made, the problems of unethical practices in the industry remain and costs continue to increase.

In light of these realities, the primary thesis of this book is that when we spend the money intended for oversight and regulatory compliance on human factor-based education at all levels of academic training and leadership development, we will minimize acts of fraudulent business practices and subsequently increase company profitability in the industry. Secondly, profitability increases in direct proportion to any improvement made to the quality of the human factor. The need for such regulatory involvement will be reduced as more people become inner-directed, as the connection between heart and mind is developed in the direction of principle-centeredness. This book provides a profitability analysis of the costs associated with industry regulations and controls from both a public policy standpoint and a corporate perspective. It is concluded that we can reduce the taxpayer's burden through a human factor-based education program in the brokerage industry.

## The Organization of This Book

With the foregoing in perspective, the remainder of this book is organized in the following manner. Chapter 1, the introduction, states clearly the purpose of this book. Chapter 2 is a presentation on the dreams and desires of those who made the formation of the United States as a nation a reality. The contents of this chapter spell out clearly these people's quest for a nation and the implications of making good on it. While Chapter 3 concentrates on the degree to which the United States government got involved in the securities industry, Chapter 4 discusses in detail the birthing process and the establishment of the securities regulations in the United States. The formation of the Securities and Exchange Commission (SEC) is also presented.

In Chapter 5, the realities of the birth of securities regulations and their implications for the shackling of Wall Street are presented and discussed. The degree to which the federal government of the United States influences business in the securities industry is discussed. The contents of Chapter 6 focus on mandated government training programs. The discussion in this chapter aims at providing answers to the pertinent question: Can these correct ethical issues? While Chapter 7 focuses on the implications of excessive government regulation, Chapter 8 tackles the idea of how to deal with the moral challenges that prevail in business. This discussion is carried out within the framework of the significance of the human factor model. Our observations and recommendations for public policy are presented and discussed in Chapter 9.

# CHAPTER 2

# The Quest for a Nation and Its Implications

THE UNITED STATES of America had a unique birth. Founded by those who felt the need for a free existence and ability to pursue life's joys on their own terms, America has always been a beacon of light around the world. America represents a place where anyone can become anything and the pursuit of happiness is implied. It is a place where any individual can have an opinion and share it without fear of persecution or prosecution. America is a place where justice is demanded and freedom is fought for and treasured.

The birth of our nation began with a trek from Europe to the new world. The journey was largely driven by people looking for an opportunity to express their faith. Many of the original colonizers were people leaving England as a protest to the establishment of the Church of England. They risked the treacherous journey across the ocean for the right to practice their own religion. They wanted to live in a place where religion could not be imposed on them by the state. Most of the people leaving England for the new world were Puritans and Roman Catholics. The Puritans who settled Massachusetts Bay believed they had a special covenant with God to establish a true Christian community. They believed that they had been chosen for this mission and that they were expected to set the standard for others to follow. The Calvert family, also known as the Earls of Baltimore, settled in Maryland with the intent of making it a "refuge for English Catholics" (Rice, Krout, & Harris, 1971, p. 18). Quakers were responsible for the settlement of Pennsylvania in an effort to practice their own religion and escape the Church of England. The Puritans settled Rhode Island and New Hampshire for religious reasons as well.

Others who came to the colonies did so for economic reasons. They were searching for opportunities and ways for their ingenuity and hard work to develop into a comfortable living for their family. These were mostly lower-class people who would only remain lower class in a caste society. Their opportunities in England, and most of Europe, would be minimal. These people were seeking prosperity through the use of their own skills, abilities, resourcefulness, and hard work.

In brief, the country that is now the United States has a proud history with very deep roots in two core beliefs:

1. Strong religious conviction and desire to practice religion freely
2. The desire to achieve economic prosperity through one's own efforts

These motivations are the foundation of what built the nation, and they are two of the main issues under attack today. The history of America makes no excuses for expression of religion. We should not be apologizing for the fact that our society is based in Judeo-Christian beliefs. It is to the credit of those original settlers that their insistence on a society of principles and ethics evolved into the strong nation we now enjoy. Our history, society, and culture are replete with examples of ethical individuals making life better for others. It is to the credit of those original settlers that our ancestors bred a people determined to create, grow, plan, and put hard work at the center of family life. Rewards of hard work were evident in the new world. Rewards in the old European society were scarce. The original colonies grew out of the backbone of hard work and were guided by the principles that made America great.

Many American communities were shaped by the churches or religious sects that dominated that particular area. They were enjoying religious freedom and economic success. For those reasons, Europeans continued to make the journey to the new world.

The Europeans enjoyed the success of the colonies as well. Initially, due to the contracts and agreements in place, much of what the colonies grew or created ended up enriching their home countries. Consequently, when the Americans objected to the oppressive taxation, the British felt forced to impose their will. When British authorities began asserting more control over the colonies, the people objected. Several laws were imposed, culminating in a revolt in 1773 referred to as the Boston Tea Party.

The American spirit was already strong, and the nature of free, independent, self-governing communities was going to be difficult to remove. It was a final straw, the Coercive Acts (referred to by the colonists as the Intolerable Acts) that forced the formation of the Continental Congress in 1774.

The stage was already set for revolt when Thomas Paine wrote a powerful pamphlet capturing the attention of the colonists. *Common Sense*, published in January of 1776, fanned the flame of separation from England. Initially most colonists wanted to assert their rights while continuing to remain a colony of England. *Common Sense*, however, made a strong argument for pure separation and independence. Some historians credit Thomas Paine with arousing that spirit that drove American independence. Paine refers to government as "a necessary evil at best and an intolerable evil at worst" (Paine, 1776, p. 1). He seemed to believe that government became necessary in order to ensure moral behavior, calling government "a mode rendered necessary by the inability of moral virtue to govern the world." In the early days of the colonies, morality was of extreme importance. Government was a method of establishing a system of expectations that could set boundaries for people; however, even with this concern, Paine cautioned that government should not become too large or invasive. He warned that the larger the size of government, the more likely it is to become disorderly. Government should remain simple, easy to comprehend, and foundational. Government from the distant shores of England and through a monarchical system was not consistent with the vision of an independent, ethical nation of freedom and equality. Paine considered monarchy evil and oppressive, and he was adamantly against hereditary succession, which inherently lacked the equal treatment and opportunity that the colonists viewed as essential.

Paine's words formed the foundation for the vision of America: "Now is the seed time of continental union, faith and honor. The reformation was preceded by the discovery of America, as if the Almighty graciously meant to open a sanctuary to the persecuted" (Paine, 1776, p. 27). Americans have always believed in their destiny as a haven for the oppressed and a beacon of hope to the persecuted.

Freedom was a driving desire for the colonists. Self-rule and self-determination were non-negotiable items. Paine, again, assisted in putting the force of his oratory to the backs of those marching forward toward independence: "Every spot of the old world is overrun with oppression. Freedom hath been haunted round the globe. Asia and Africa have long expelled her. Europe regards her like a stranger, and England hath given her warning to depart. O! Receive the fugitive and prepare in time for an asylum for mankind" (Paine, 1776, p. 42).

The Declaration of Independence was signed on July 4, 1776, announcing America's intention to leave the fold of the British Empire. The basis of the Declaration was that all men are created equal and endowed by the Creator with certain rights: life, liberty, and the pursuit of happiness. With this basic foundation for society and government, the colonists were establishing a nation like none before it.

The British, of course, rejected the entire idea and, instead, moved to restore their domination with the British army. The Declaration of Independence became the War for Independence. The British thought it was a minor uprising that could be easily squelched. The resilience of the Patriots came as a surprise, and the length of the war became a problem. With far fewer men, supplies, guns, ammunition, money and anything else normally needed for war, the Continental Army prevailed against all odds. Motivated by principles of faith, freedom, and a sense of destiny and purpose, the colonists became independent Americans.

After winning her independence from Great Britain, America controlled her destiny through wars with the Indians, Mexicans, and French. The new leadership negotiated for more land and expanded commerce, and built a nation with perseverance and purpose. The Louisiana Purchase opened up new territory, and America became a nation of immigrants. People from all over Europe arrived through Ellis Island and dispersed from the shores of New York across the plains and into the fertile valleys of the West. Americans conquered the West, built industry in the South, and became a good friend and economic partner to its former colonizers. America was truly a free and faithful nation.

Throughout the 18th century, America was immersed in developing all the qualities that the original forefathers envisioned during the signing of the Declaration of Independence and developed through the writing of the United States Constitution. The leaders of the nation established laws and court systems. They developed infrastructure and organizations. Taxation, trade, and forms of commerce were considered. In short, the country put meat on the bones of the original idea of America.

They discovered areas of disagreement. Issues such as slavery, states' rights, and representation were viewed differently from one state to another. In the 1860s, the disagreements that seemed to place the North and the South on opposite sides erupted. This escalation resulted in the Civil War when the South tried to cede from the union and President Abraham Lincoln refused to accept the disintegration of the nation. A very bloody war was fought, pitting brothers against brothers and fathers against sons, but in the end, the union, and all that it represented and promised, prevailed.

After fighting an internal war, the United States had no appetite for involvement in the affairs of Europe. Regardless, eventually World War I interrupted the isolationism that America was enjoying. Finding it nearly impossible to remain neutral in the face of blockades, sunken ships, and trade disruptions, the United States entered World War I in April 1917. Woodrow Wilson stated that the aggression of Germany was intolerable, and thus he sent American troops to bolster the British and the French. With the Americans fully engaged on the side of the Allies, the tide swiftly turned against Germany and its supporters. The Americans helped bring an end to the war quickly while at the same time changing the course of their own history as well as the perception of America abroad.

At the end of the war, peace returned, and along with it came a resurgence of interest in commerce and economics. America entered a period of prosperity, and it is at this point in our history that the securities industry emerged and investment brokers became ubiquitous in the financial transactions of day-to-day life. This is the beginning of the history of the securities industry and regulatory involvement.

# CHAPTER 3

# It was the Best of Times that Became the Worst of Times...

WHEN MOST PEOPLE think about the 1920s in America, visions brought to mind are flappers, gangsters, and prohibitions. Movies set in the 1920s show men with pinstripe suits and hats perched rakishly atop a head and above a dark glare. Women are portrayed at the beginning of the women's movement testing their independence by smoking cigarettes publicly for the first time. They shocked the world with dramatic new hairstyles and glamorous clothes that made fashion an industry. Jazz music was everywhere, and dancing the Charleston was the rage. News from that period was largely concerned with the raids on speakeasy establishments and the battle over prohibitions. The government was obsessed with eradicating the evils of drinking and pursued every avenue possible to combat those who had become lawbreakers with one swipe of the president's pen.

The 1920s were a peaceful time. After World War I, those returning from war were fortunate to be alive, and many celebrated in small ways every day. Warren Harding campaigned in favor of a return to Americanism and away from internationalism, while his Democratic opponent, James Cox, advocated for the League of Nations, encouraging a national citizenry and a place in the world's political community. Americans, tired of the war and desirous of a return to peaceful isolationism, voted overwhelmingly Republican, 61% to 35% Democrat (DeGregorio, 2002, p. 438). Harding became president, and the country flourished.

While Americans were enjoying peace, prosperity, and jazz, largely ignored at the time were the activities on Wall Street and in the securities industry, and perhaps in business as a whole. The political approach to business had been a combination of *caveat emptor* and *laissez-faire*. Businesspeople enjoyed lowered tax rates on corporations and growth of the post-war economy.

In the midst of the drinking, dancing, and economic prosperity, Americans were caught completely off guard when the market crashed in 1929. They looked to Washington and discovered that government leaders were just as unprepared for the consequences of that event and the economic depression that followed.

## Pre-Depression

### The Pre-Regulatory Roaring '20s

Prior to the depression, the federal government had virtually no involvement in the securities industry. There was no oversight, no regulation, and very few rules to govern the stock market. It was a free market economy, and there were few complaints about that until the stock market crashed. Until this time, people who invested in the stock market saw their income grow. They saw returns on their investments, and the only question was, by how much? The expectation of a loss on the market was minimal, and the entire crash seemed impossible. During the 1920s, the stock market rose consistently: "Many began to believe that the rise would be permanent and the growth curve would be unending" (Sobel, 1968, p. 21).

Logically, this made sense to people. After World War I, the country experienced unprecedented prosperity. Those who returned from war found the economic opportunities were endless, and many previously struggling families were able to purchase homes, joining the ranks of the middle class: "The nation was engaged in a great expansion, profits were rising and conditions seemed sound" (Sobel,

1968, p. 21). Soldiers returning from war found that the recessionary conditions they left had been replaced by growth and progress. The demand for American goods was high, and the war had actually boosted American exports to Europe: "The gross domestic product (GNP) of 1919 was $41.8 billion. The nation's export balance in 1918 was $6.2 billion and in 1919 it was a record $7.9 billion" (Sobel, 1968, p. 24). With so many new investors on Wall Street, it was not difficult to imagine the confusion that ensued once the market began to move in a downward trend. The business cycle often resulted in various changes in the market, both upwards and downwards, but those who saw only prosperity expected only prosperity.

In 1919, there was a labor shortage, and anyone interested in working was able to find a job easily. In a capitalist society, this meant opportunity for those willing to work hard. Compared to the other countries involved in World War I, the United States did not suffer the devastation of its economy and neighborhood decay. The United States did not have reconstruction needs, and the business community was poised to step in to fill the needs of a consumer marketplace that previously had been dominated by the Europeans.

With the major players in Europe exhausted from war and consumed with the necessary activities to return country and countrymen back to some level of comfort, losing market share to the Americans was of little concern: "Having attained the upper hand over the domestic reformers, and now the leading commercial factor in the world, the American businessman was the only major victor of the world war" (Sobel, 1968, p. 24). The optimism in the country and the expectation of ongoing prosperity drove people to Wall Street in droves. The market was rising to unprecedented levels, and many people wanted to be a part of the excitement. New investors, arguably inexperienced investors, entered the market in large numbers at this time.

## The Devil of Debt Culture

The market share that Americans had acquired during and after World War I, however, began to disappear as the European effort

12

to rebuild their businesses and competition became fierce: "By December 1919, the analysts noted that the American exchanges had not shown the strength of their European counterparts" (Sobel, 1968, p. 25). The other growing threat was the high level of debt Americans had begun accepting. By 1927, the American people had become comfortable with the concept of consumer credit. Previously it took time to save and earn the right to make a large consumer purchase. With the new concept of *buying on time*, consumers were able to buy much sooner than they had planned or even dreamed. Items that had been out of reach for most families became possible with the emergence of the new debt culture. Before long, many items were bought through installment contracts. For example, in 1927, 80% of all phonographs, 75% of all washing machines, and more than half of other large items were bought on credit (Sobel, 1968, p. 45). Debt continued to grow as consumers realized how easy it was to get what they wanted quickly by just signing a contract.

As consumer credit became more popular, a parallel paradigm shift was taking place on Wall Street. If consumers could buy a radio on credit, why couldn't an investor buy a stock on margin? Financial instruments designed to encourage consumers to live beyond their means became accepted and used, in some cases, recklessly. Along with the acceptance of debt came the acceptance of risk. The likelihood of losing money in the stock market seemed farfetched. Investing on margin seemed simple and easy. Individuals began buying stocks on margin in large numbers. This left a great deal of money at risk. Although there was significant growth in the stock market and consumer purchasing along with a large price tag of debt attached, the government took no interest. The viewpoint at this time was that business was best left alone. Economic growth was good for the country, and if Wall Street was fueling it, then the government did not interfere. That was the prevailing philosophy.

In the early 1920s, Andrew Mellon was the U.S. treasury secretary. With a business background and a family of influential business leaders, he was interested in continuing the growth of the economy and the expansion of business. Andrew Mellon became the secretary of treasury with goals of reducing the government debt. He had a firm belief that if people felt that taxes were unfair, they would simply find ways to avoid paying them. If most people could see the logic and reasoning, and if there were a just system in place for taxation, people would accept the payment of taxes as part of the responsibility of good citizenship. During his tenure, government expenditures were cut, and the surpluses were used to pay off portions of the national debt. He was quoted as stating, "The Government is just a business and can and should be run on business principles" (Sobel, 1968, p. 51). He was committed to keeping government small while containing public costs and providing a climate of freedom in which it would be likely that business could thrive and grow.

While it seems almost inconceivable in the current day, Secretary Mellon was able to reduce the public debt while decreasing taxes for all Americans. He often was quoted explaining his view of the *immorality* of heavy taxes (Sobel, 1968, p. 52). As Mellon wrote in 1924, "The history of taxation shows that taxes which are inherently excessive are not paid. The high rates inevitably put pressure upon the taxpayer to withdraw his capital from productive business" (*Wikipedia*, retrieved 5/17). Mellon felt that taxes could be reduced and maintained at a low level if government used taxpayer money wisely and if the government functioned efficiently. Mellon agreed with the general theory that the right thing to do is to have a progressive taxation system where lower-wage earners pay less in taxes, but for him, top income earners could not be overburdened. His quest for justice in taxation was clear. He made a clear distinction between *earned* income and *unearned* income, believing in the fairness of taxing income from wages more lightly than those from inheritance or other sources. He stated, "Surely we can afford to make a distinction between the people whose only capital is their mettle and physical energy and the people whose income is derived from investments" (Mellon, 1924). He understood that individuals have a certain finite number of productive years where they can take care of their own families and prepare for the years when they are no longer able to earn income.

Prior to the Great Depression, there was little interest in curbing the voracious appetite the American consumer had developed for participating in the stock market. A few bills were proposed in Congress, but none of any significance was ever passed. Most people were not concerned about the amount of money they had dependent upon increasing stock prices, and very few constraints were considered. While most of the power brokers in Washington were content to let the business community function unfettered, there were a few rumblings and some concerns about what was going on in the securities industry. There were a few speaking out about the danger of margin buying and large amounts of debt rapidly accumulating in both companies and families.

The Investment Bankers Association (IBA) was a national organization trying to ensure proper standards for the financial sector. While a few states were implementing controls on sales of securities products, the Investment Bankers Association tried to get support for national standards. The IBA warned of the potential risks of market volatility and irresponsibility of both investors and brokers. It was concerned about the ethics of the financial advisors entrusted with the savings of unsuspecting Americans. L.B. Lawrence of Guaranty Trust once observed, "Millions upon millions of the savings of people of moderate means are each year falling into the clutches of the get-rich-quick promoter and the bucket shop" (Parrish, 1970, p. 8). Lawrence asked the IBA to be more proactive in getting legislation passed to guide the business, and he encouraged far more education and training for those responsible for selling investment products (Parrish, 1970, p. 8). He had support among some of the IBA leaders.

W.H.J. Maxwell, Jr. of the IBA's fraudulent advising committee noted, "In no years in the past have these people [fraudulent dealers] been so bold and so unscrupulous" (Parrish, 1970, p. 15). He explained that due to the lack of oversight and legislation, anyone who had the desire to be unscrupulous in his or her dealings with the

American public certainly had the ability to do so. While there was much excitement about the rise of values on Wall Street, there was no way of knowing what was going on behind the scenes. Without any auditors or checkpoints, it was very easy to sell fraudulent stocks and bonds, and by the time anyone would discover these doubtful securities, it would be too late (Parrish, 1970, p. 15).

The problem seemed to be that as long as it was easy to do things the wrong way, some found no reason to do things the right way. With a healthy (i.e., positive) human factor, regardless of regulations, individuals would choose to do what is in the best interest of the client. Audits and checkpoints would be unnecessary. The decay of the human factor already seemed evident at this point.

The human factor includes six components: spiritual capital, moral capital, aesthetic capital, human capital, human abilities, and the human potential (Adjibolosoo, 1995, p. 33-38). It will be answered in this book that if individuals were to grow in the positive qualities of the human factor, they would feel compelled to behave in a manner reflective of a healthy human factor. The decay of the human factor would cause people to behave as described during the pre-regulatory years. It is also argued that those without a healthy human factor will make decisions and choices reflective of that condition regardless of any regulatory authority. Laws and regulations are a challenge, not prevention. The contents of this book will show that it is time to look for a better way to address corruption and unscrupulous practices in the brokerage industry.

Although the IBA continued to pressure for federal regulations, as severe human factor decay continued to dog trading activities on Wall Street, there was no enthusiasm for government intervention at this point. A new IBA president took over, essentially declaring the battle over and the issue dead. In 1927, Pliny Jewell, IBA president, stated, "There is no need of Federal legislation....With most of the states already with adequate specific laws, with the assistance of the postal authorities and our basic common law...nothing further is needed" (Parrish, 1970, p. 20). While some were still concerned, nothing would be done to monitor the securities industry at this point. The real challenge of severe human factor decay was swept under the carpet and given a long leash to ferment, only to emerge later and larger with a harsh impact for a new, unsuspecting public. Without addressing the human factor decay, the door was left open to promote fraudulent and deceitfulness on Wall Street.

## Reckless Recruitment

Another change that began during the post-war decade of prosperity was the expansion of the companies servicing clients with stock purchases. As many more individuals became investors, there was a demand for financial services. More brokerage houses opened, and more financial advisors were hired. Prior to the growth period, becoming a financial advisor was considered quite an honor. These men were well respected, as they had to earn the right to be considered for any position as a financial advisor. Very few broker positions existed, and few people knew the business of securities brokerage. With rapid expansion came quick recruitment and hiring. Many new companies sold securities, and people who might otherwise never be considered eligible were promoted to the exclusive ranks of financial advisor very quickly.

With literally hundreds of openings, many people vied for the positions. Branch offices, new firms, and the growth of research facilities caused the demand for positions to outstrip the supply of talent (Sobel, 1968, p. 64). In addition to the typical candidates, many newcomers, attracted by glamour and the hope for easy, large incomes, joined the financial advisor community. In some cases, these were people "whose talents were more suited to the race track or bucket shops" (Sobel, 1968, p. 64). Bucket shops were illegal brokerage firms run by unethical members. These types of individuals would never have been even considered for reputable brokerage firms in the past.

Typical training for new brokers consisted of a two-week course on stock market techniques, after which they were provided with a desk and the ability to invest large sums of money for their clients (Sobel,

1968, p. 65). With very little experience, minimal background, and, more often than not, questionable motives and ethics, those staffing the brokerage houses at this time did not always have the best interest of their clients at heart. What may have been done with knowledge and good intentions was now done with greed and selfishness. This influx of inexperienced and unethical employees began a trend of morally questionable practices in the brokerage industry that continued and that have been in evidence ever since. While efforts have been made to exclude unethical brokers, there continue to be those unscrupulous few who find their way into the industry.

In the summer of 1929, there was a warning raised in some publications noting the inflated common-stock values of many companies on the exchange. This warning was disregarded, as most people interpreted the warning as only applicable to *speculation* and not general investing (deBedtz, 1964, p. 10). Although there were some concerns about insider trading, there was no law against it and, up until this point, no one had suffered because of it. President Herbert Hoover commented on this, saying, "I stated that I preferred to let American institutions and the states govern themselves, and that the exchange had full power under its charter to control its own members, and to prevent it from being used for manipulation against the public interest" (deBedtz, 1964, p. 12). Generally reflecting the feeling of his time, President Hoover believed that American businesspeople could be trusted to do what is in the best interest of the public and that they should be left alone to conduct business without the interference of the federal government. President Hoover did, however, warn that if it became problematic and if the industry could no longer be trusted to govern itself, then federal regulation would become inevitable (deBedtz, 1964, p. 13).

Regardless of their lack of experience, many of these new brokers were deemed successful initially. In spite of their lack of formal education, knowledge, and skill, the bull market during the 1920s made it easy to pick stocks, sit back, and watch them increase in value. For several years, consequently, the inexperienced brokers flew under the radar, and most people felt confident in their positions on Wall Street. The combination of inexperienced brokers and inexperienced investors, however, proved to be detrimental. While most investors expected only positive returns, inexperienced brokers were also unaware of the possible consequences of a bear market. Clients were not warned that their investments could lose value, and brokers did not prepare for the possibilities of an overall correction in the market. There were concerns that not all business on Wall Street was being conducted with the high levels of integrity that should be expected particularly with the responsibility of a financial advisor: investing the savings and retirement monies of others who trust him. Clearly, the challenges of severe human factor decay continue to emerge and entrench themselves on Wall Street.

President-elect Hoover noted, "Our whole business system would break down in a day if there was not a high sense of moral responsibility in our business world" (deBetz, 1964, p. 13) as he warned against over-indulgence in Wall Street's alluring draw. Arguably, by this time the presence of severe human factor decay on Wall Street had become an open secret. With the availability of margin accounts and the excessive amount of leverage used, the situation was unstable. Brokers were willing to loan clients the money to invest and, without any controls or safeguards, irresponsible leaders of Wall Street made some aggressive decisions largely out of their own greed, in addition to ignorance. As ever, the attention was on the instruments of speculation. Nothing was said or done about the decisive factor, the tendency to speculation itself. Somewhat belatedly, efforts were made to remove incompetent and shady brokers, and those brokers deemed to be worthy of the responsibilities of the position were required to accept and live by an ethical code of conduct. These efforts, however, were too little and too late. Until this point, severe human factor decay had already taken residence on Wall Street. Crooked agents were more than willing to provide the opportunity it required to express itself in market dealings and trading.

# CHAPTER 4

# The Post-depression Years

THE GREAT DEPRESSION was a turning point in American history for a number of reasons, one of which was the newfound interest in government oversight and involvement in the activities of private investors on Wall Street. When the stock market crashed in 1929, approximately half of the wealth of the country evaporated. Active investors, who had previously thrived by entering the market, saw their entire fortunes disappear before their very eyes. The Great Depression began with unpredictably higher levels of unemployment. Within a very short period of time, a stunning 4 million people were out of work and almost half a million independent farmers lost their homes. The lack of income caused approximately 100,000 bankruptcies, and people were desperate for food and shelter.

Sounding eerily similar to 2007, the depression of 1927 began with people increasing their debt by investing more on margin and making consumer purchases on credit. While the extensive consumer debt was problematic, the large margin accounts in the stock market had dire consequences. As individuals lost their jobs and their investments in the stock market at the same time, families lost income as well as savings, resulting in complete financial devastation. By the end of October 1929, after years of consistent upward trends, the market took its precipitous fall and eventually collapsed. On October 24, 1929, more than $9 billion in paper value was wiped out; leaving many people "dazed, confused, and broke" (Sobel, 1968, p. 135). Panic began to set in among corporate leaders and Main Street investors. Margin calls went out to homes and businesses across the country. While people had become very comfortable with debt, they had no plan to cover the amount they had on margin. Embarrassed to admit they were unprepared, individual investors were desperate for help.

In some segments, the October 1929 crash was blamed on risky investments and speculation. Because the securities market had been *self-regulating*, the market was deemed to be *leaderless*. As a result, leadership was difficult to find when problems began occurring. Without a clear leader, individual, or group, there was confusion in the effort to find and appoint responsibility. The stock exchange was considered partly to blame because of the excesses of short-selling and buying on margin. The head of the exchange blamed the public. He stated that the American people purchased on margin and without a great deal of knowledge, which was considered their own fault. The American public blamed the *slick salesmen*. They defended their *wild speculation* as a response to the aggressive selling techniques and persuasive practices of the high-powered brokers that pitched the stock purchases (deBedtz, 1964, p. 19).

Yet, regardless of what the blame was pinned down on, few people were aware that the challenges of fraudulent practices on Wall Street were fueled by severe human factor decay. Unfortunately, few leaders and players were readily willing to acknowledge the contributions of the severe human factor decay to the challenges in the stock market. While leaders as well as citizens played the blame game, severe human factor decay had a field day. Unchecked and unrestrained, it entrenched itself and led market makers to serve according to the drive of ambition, greed, and power. Wall Street prayed to the money god and served its idol religiously, becoming devout in its addiction to adrenaline and the lure of power. A Gordon Gekko line in the movie "Wall Street" rings true: Gekko starts his presentation with "Greed is good." He repeats the line again, looking around the room to ensure that everyone is paying attention. The room full of blue suits and white shirts looked enraptured. Early on, Wall Street became devoutly committed to greed. Greed became a piece of the poison injected into a system already suffering from human factor decay.

According to John Kenneth Galbraith, the cause of the crash resulted from *speculation and financial euphoria*. He believed that Americans were overly optimistic about the stock market and were either uninformed or refused to consider realities: "The price of the object of speculation goes up. Securities, land, objets d'art, and other property, when bought today, are worth more tomorrow. This increase, and the prospect of continued increases, attracts new buyers; the new buyers then assure a further increase. More are attracted, more buy and the speculation building on itself provides its own momentum" (Galbraith, 1990, p. 3). As the momentum continued, more people jumped into the market, driving prices up. Once something triggered a decrease, investors started selling, and the momentum went in the opposite direction. Like lemmings, investors followed one another off the financial cliff. Galbraith believed the attitude of investors was the root cause of a market crash and that the attitudes of people participating in the market tended to have the impact that drove the market. That is why news commentators refer to the *mood of investors*. There is an impact felt by perception, or the feelings of the individual investor.

According to Galbraith, there are two types of people who invest in the market. The first is those who are persuaded that some new circumstance is going to allow them to benefit and that this new twist will result in their rapid rise to wealth. They expect that the market will just keep going up, resulting in continued returns. The second group of people does not believe that the market will keep going up. They do not believe in perfect circumstances that will result in wealth. They do believe, however, that their own skill and intelligence will result in experiencing wealth due to their choice of speculative investments. They believe that their *particular genius* will allow them to ride the tide upwards and yet have the instinct to jump out before the fall. We might simplify it by saying one type of investor is naive and the other is arrogant. As Galbraith says, "Built into this situation is the eventual and inevitable fall" (Galbraith, 1990, p. 4).

## Political Influence

The country was in trouble, and there was public outcry. What was largely emotional rather than logical at the time was a sense of desperation and strong feeling that the government needed to provide safeguards and oversight. Many concerns were raised, ranging from the quality of the brokers and their ethical standards to the functioning of broker/dealers and the excessive margin accounts of individual consumers. All over the country there were claims of *rotten securities* and *unethical brokers*. When President Hoover became genuinely concerned about the possibility of a lack of integrity in a small segment of the market, he initiated an investigation into all "practices with respect to buying and selling and borrowing and lending of listed securities." The question was asked, not about how to manage the exchange, but if regulation was to be necessary. In obvious support of this need brought upon by the October 1929 crash, Congress appropriated significant funds for this investigation (deBedtz, 1968, p. 17).

During the course of this investigation, it quickly became evident that not all was bright and shiny on Wall Street. There were certainly some questionable activities, and the integrity of the people involved in the marketplace was no longer a given: "Recognition of those frauds and abuses just emerging from the Senate investigation formed an important plank in the Democratic party platform" (deBedtz, 1968, p. 24). President Hoover was tasked with explaining the activities of Wall Street, and the timing could not have been worse for his political future. This issue, of course, became a rallying cry during the election of 1932. A major campaign theme surrounded the securities industry, highlighting the differences between Hoover, the Republican in favor of small government and a free, capitalist economy, and Roosevelt, the Democrat promising government support for public services, such as aid to farmers and senior citizens.

Roosevelt promised shorter working hours and much more public support for individuals. His campaign stump speeches included attacks on business, and he insisted that, if elected, he would provide federal regulation of securities as well as utilities and restrictions on banking. The terms of the debate were clear.

The Democratic Party platform included statements about the protection of the investing public and a proposal for full regulation and oversight provided by the federal government, and this became part of the political debate between Hoover and Roosevelt. Roosevelt largely criticized Hoover for his hands-off approach toward business, and he insisted that more needed to be done to reign in the activities on Wall Street. Roosevelt made statements referring to his opponent and his administration by describing them as "[u]nsound investing policies under a lax and indifferent leader" (deBedtz 1964, p. 27). Roosevelt made it clear that if he were elected, he would differ significantly from his predecessor in the handling of the securities industry. While Hoover had held firm in his belief that doctrine of *caveat emptor* should continue to rule business in general and Wall Street in particular, Roosevelt expected the government to have oversight authority and the ability to control certain aspects of business. He made it clear that, in his opinion, government should be legislating and regulating activity to protect consumers against what, according to deBedtz, Roosevelt referred to as "practices neither ethical nor honest on the part of many persons or corporations selling securities" (deBedtz, 1964, p. 33).

Roosevelt felt it was important to bring back the confidence of the investing public. He expected that business could only continue to thrive in the United States if people felt that they were going to be treated fairly, honestly, and ethically. According to deBedtz, Roosevelt stated the following in his public papers referring to the regulation of the securities industry:

This is but one step in our broad purpose of protecting investors and depositors. It should be followed by legislation relating to better supervision of the purchase and sale of all property dealt in on the exchanges, and the legislation to correct unethical and unsafe practices on the part of officers and directors of banks and other corporations. (deBedtz, 1964, p. 34)

Among Roosevelt's supporters were many people who felt they had been lied to and cheated out of their investments. They wanted retribution and punishment for any practices in the industry they viewed as unethical and lacking integrity. Wall Street had developed an image of greed and a perception of dishonesty that would be hard to shake. Those who lost money in the market were not going to forgive and forget very easily. The public sentiment put pressure on the leadership, influenced the election, and caused a new role for government with unprecedented power and authority previously considered inconceivable in a capitalist economy.

## The Debate

The presidential debate mirrored conversations on street corners and in diners across the country. People on Main Street were starting to believe that they had been taken advantage of by greedy people on Wall Street. As experts began theorizing about the causes, arguments were made that the crash could have been avoided by implementing regulations and instituting guidelines for the sale of investment products. It was theorized that if the IBA or the New York Stock Exchange had more controls, they could have stopped greedy and predatory practices. One side of the discussion made the clear connection between government regulations and safety in the securities industry. This position was backed by prominent voices such as presidential candidate Franklin D. Roosevelt. Roosevelt came on strong and fed off the public passion for persecution of the securities industry in his campaigning. Few focused on the quality of the country's citizens and the decaying human factor. Repair of the human factor would have been an attempt to minimize the downward cycle of reckless and irresponsible behavior that would have sent Wall Street down a different path. The severe human factor decay was not effectively addressed. The public was demanding a legal/governmental response instead.

Some prominent individuals, however, did not believe regulatory response was the proper approach. Arthur H. Dean, for example, commented on the plans to reshape Wall Street by stating that "it hardly seems necessary to burn down the house to exterminate the vermin" (deBedtz, 1964, p. 52). His position, like many others, reflected a more moderate viewpoint: that, while there were certainly some unethical brokers and employees in the business, the entire business as a whole should not be painted with such a broad brush.

While there was agreement that there were problems on Wall Street, there was no uniformity in the method of attempting to correct the problems. Although some unfortunate individuals lost a great deal of money, many also earned large returns from their investments on Wall Street. Investors wanted to have their cake and eat it too. They wanted to participate in the bull market but have the government rush in and take control in the bear market. They wanted insurance against any negative consequence, while fully enjoying the benefits of all the healthy returns during the good years. This philosophy did not seem to fit with the common understanding of a free market and capitalist society. The New Deal meant a very new direction for the country, particularly as it related to business and the securities industry. The voting public made a statement reflective of their feelings at the time, at least in part due to their recent experiences with Wall Street. Roosevelt won the election of 1932 with 57% of the popular vote to Hoover's 40% (DeGregorio, 2002, p. 487).

Largely due to the public's perception of what was happening to society, the Republicans lost control of the White House in 1932, turning the country over to a Democratic administration bent on social programs and government involvement. The Democrats were able to capitalize on the disappointment and concerns of individuals and, consequently, they won the election easily. Most people wanted to have problems dealt with, and they expected change. The Democrats promised help for the consumer while the Republicans did not believe government solutions were the answer. The public was tired and looking for a new direction. While the two sides reflected very different solutions, neither addressed the human factor issues.

Human factor–based education includes the six components of the human factor. These components include spiritual capital, moral capital, aesthetic capital, human capital, human abilities, and the human potential (Adjibolosoo, 1995, p. 33-38). According to Adjibolosoo, in order to develop quality leaders in business or in government, those involved in the leadership development programs must concentrate on qualities such as love, joy, peace, patience, kindness, goodness, faithfulness, gentleness, and self-control (Adjibolosoo, 2005, p. 44).

With these realities in mind, problems in the brokerage industry, including fraud, irresponsible attitudes, and unethical behavior, cannot be corrected by adding laws, new regulations, and additional regulatory bodies. More bureaucracy and additional oversight will not correct the real problem of severe human factor decay. In the remainder of this book, we propose that in order to minimize corruption in the business community, it is imperative to address the problem of severe human factor decay in the industry and in the country. Only when this is addressed effectively can we expect to make the long-lasting changes and meaningful improvement that will result in consistent, ethical business practices.

# CHAPTER 5

# Government Involvement

PRESIDENT ROOSEVELT TOOK office in 1932 and immediately went to work fulfilling his promises. As part of the correction of the Depression and the New Deal, oversight of the securities industry became a high priority. The Depression changed America's perception of the free market and the concept of wealth generation through stock market investments. During the government's investigation, it became clear that there was so much competition among investment bankers that they failed to apply ethical approaches and sensible actions to their practices. In the effort to secure more significant market share, integrity was compromised. There was evidence that investment houses issued false and misleading prospectuses. International bonds provided lavish commissions. Bankers ignored poor debt records while enthusiastically supporting and soliciting sales of bonds (Parrish, 1970, p. 75).

The more details that emerged about the activities on Wall Street, the more resolute President Roosevelt became in establishing a set of regulations to provide some protection to the American consumer. He continued to seek the involvement of experts in the industry to craft appropriate legislation. At one point, he referred to the people managing the stock exchange as in dire need of an elementary education. He described the lack of education this way: "I do not mean a college diploma, but the inability to understand the country of the public or their obligation to their fellow men" (Parrish, 1970, p. 109). With these words he seemed to be addressing more than their lack of education. It went so far as to the very basic understanding of personal responsibility and integrity. In recommending legislation for federal supervision of traffic in investment securities, he announced the effort by stating, "Such legislation should give impetus to honest dealing...and thereby bring back public confidence" (Parrish, 1970, p. 47). Roosevelt was interested in the cause of the collapse as well as the solution, but he also seemed to put individual responsibility at the forefront of the expectations of the industry.

One of the primary leaders of this effort was Huston Thompson. He was a strong supporter *of the Sherman Antitrust Act* and believed fiercely in American independence and the abilities of competitive capitalist systems. In tackling this issue, he framed the discussion with the understanding that too much government involvement would be disastrous but that laws properly applied could encourage competition and protect entrepreneurial freedom. He was very much against any expansion of the government bureaucracy and wanted to keep the new regulations simple. He feared the "erosion of economic individualism, which he associated with personal morality, dignity and initiative" (Parrish, 1970, p. 46).

## Function and Dysfunction of Congress

Some of the challenges in crafting this legislation, however, are chronic conditions that have not disappeared. Once the proposed law was sent to Congress, it became mired in controversy and grandstanding. Some lawmakers just wanted to delay the process in order to help their backers on Wall Street, and some congressmen desired to put their palm print on the regulations for the purpose of their own recognition. As usual, there were turf wars and power struggles. Further evidence of a decaying human factor became clear even in the process of correcting the perceived corruption on Wall Street. Congressional leaders had then, as they do now, more to gain or lose than just improving the lives of the American people. The members of

Congress are very driven to maintain their privileged position. In what has become an American oligarchy, these chosen few can make laws that they never have to live by.

American congressmen are very committed to keeping their jobs. It makes sense when you consider the value of the perks versus the amount of real work, compared to what the average American employee can expect. According to Dick Morris, in 2007, the House of Representatives worked only three five-day workweeks in the entire year. They tried to commit to working at least until 2 p.m. on days they do convene, but that is a goal, not a promise. The Senate did not have any five-day workweeks in 2007 (Morris, 2008, p. 88). The actual time allocated to the people's business is so minimal, and yet they seem to wreak so much havoc.

Congressmen and women can raise money each time they run for their office, and many have run far too many times. During the time they are running a campaign, they rarely manage to get to *work* in Washington. When Senators John McCain, Barack Obama, and Hillary Clinton were running for president, for example, each of them had a recorded attendance of only five days in the first three months of 2008 (Morris, 2008, p. 88). As Dick Morris points out, that is an unprecedented record of absenteeism that would never be tolerated in the private sector. Regardless of their attendance, or lack thereof, they continue to collect their taxpayer-funded salary. In the words of Dick Morris, "Would you still get paid if you took a year or two off to compete for another job?" (Morris, 2008, p. 89). On the plus side, the fact that they work so little is probably one of the only reasons the country has not sunk into complete and total disrepair at this point. The process in Congress is indicative of a spirit driven by greed, power, and self-centeredness and a very poor human factor. A healthy human factor would result in different behaviors in Congress as well as on Wall Street. It seems like the blind leading the blind for the self-centered congressional leaders to be correcting unethical behaviors of Wall Street leaders.

Those tasked with the overhaul of Wall Street in the 1930s were under a great deal of pressure from a highly agitated and attentive public. Roosevelt had made a promise to the American people, and he intended to honor his word. During the first hundred days of his presidency, he pushed an enormous amount of legislation through Congress. As a result, the quantity and pace of all the congressional activity had a negative impact on the drafting and passage of *the Securities Act* (Parrish, 1970, p. 112). Much was completed but not all was done with the thoroughness that would have provided better results in the long term. Speed was necessary to quell the complaints of the public, thus ensuring re-election for many congressmen and setting the stage for a Roosevelt re-election.

Congress also had to contend with the *dictatorship* of the powerful Chairman of the Interstate and Foreign Commerce Committee. Sam Rayburn, who eventually became a commanding Speaker of the House, was at the center of much of the New Deal legislation, and he became the individual who sponsored the federal securities act that resulted in the Securities and Exchange Commission (Cheney, 1983, p. 168). His strong hand, however, influenced the debate and prevented a beneficial discussion. One of the main objections to the initial bill was that it was based solely on economics and did not address the important social and moral judgments. Consequently, the demand was again made for control over credit on exchange trading and oversight for individual exchange members (Parrish 1970, p. 116).

One congressman complained that the bill, as it had been drafted, was an act of vengeance and an effort to punish people dealing in the securities business. There were arguments around the quality of those employed in the industry. Congressman Paul Shields, in protesting to Sam Rayburn, stated, "There are honest, decent people in this business and such people should not be destroyed" (Parrish, 1970, p. 129). According to one columnist, the bill as proposed was likely to "separate men in Government and men out of Government into two opposing camps, which is most unfortunate for a people" (Parrish, 1970, p. 129). There were essentially two camps. One believed in very active government involvement, and the other was very much against any bureaucratic encumbrances to the business sector. Today we would probably still recognize those two groups as the Democrats and Republicans. With the expansion of government and the ongoing high levels of unemployment in the private sector, the divide between government workers, particularly unions, and private sector employees has deepened again in the current time.

The other frustration experienced in passing the legislation was the lack of understanding of those expected to provide input and eventually vote for or against. With the exception of a few, most of the congressmen involved in the committee revising the bill were not considered well prepared to deal with securities-related issues. They, instead, responded to the lobbyists and those who assisted them in their elections, such as exchange presidents, traders, and other businessmen. Recognizing this, Chairman Sam Rayburn made the decision to avoid the confrontation and significantly reduced the impact of the legislation in order to get it completed. Without a great deal of industry knowledge, but with a significant amount of pressure, laws were passed.

## Invitation into the Industry

The specter of the 1930s seems to be haunting us in the current day. As it was then and as it is now, some leaders in Congress are anxious to take credit for correcting something in order to gain public affection. The popular decision overwhelms common sense. They want to ensure that they keep their favored position in Washington, and they want to be hailed as heroes in their home districts. This issue represents the perfect opportunity for loud leaders to grab the podium and stand up on their soapbox, allegedly in the interest of the defrauded consumer.

The American public demanded a response from their legislators, and the legislators acted. Whether it was effective or not was yet to be determined. Americans have a belief in our legal system and, as Roosevelt came to office, they assigned him the title of *savior*. In addition to laws, we give omnipotent power to a system of laws and legal people. While some people accept that a capitalist system has risks and inherent ups and downs, others look for a rescue or bailout when something does not go their way. Americans were perfectly happy to enjoy the gains of a bull market, but they were completely intolerant of the bear market. Regardless of the illogic of this, Roosevelt felt it important to act, securing his role as *savior*.

Given that those handling the discussion and crafting the legislation had little or no understanding of the industry, it certainly made their efforts suspect. As requested, however, the federal government responded, and government intervention has had a hand in every part of the industry ever since. Now every transaction includes the partnership of the federal government and Big Brother, and each decision is plagued with paperwork courtesy of the same. Licensing, continuing education, and training requirements are all dictated by the federal government. Consumer demands after the stock market crash of 1929 essentially created the federal oversight that is now an integral part of the landscape.

The way in which Roosevelt took charge and in which Congress stepped in satisfied many Americans. They felt that they had been listened to and, to some degree, vindicated. They believed that Wall Street players had been punished and would be under constraints in the future, unable to engage in fraudulent or questionable practices. This response from the U.S. government is reflective of the American belief in the application of legal solutions to the challenges of severe human factor decay. Americans have always had a strong belief in the rule of law and a commitment to a fair and just legal system. Our founding fathers took great pains to ensure that Americans would be treated fairly and protected from tyranny and abuse. From that time, as a nation, we have neither hidden from nor relented in our tenacity regarding our strong belief in using the law to solve the severe moral challenges that face us. In what follows in this chapter, a presentation is made in relation to the genesis of the law as the main solution to our ethical and moral problems, whose causes are actually found in severe human factor decay.

# New Direction

It was under the Roosevelt administration that the *Truth-in-Securities* legislation became the *Securities Act of 1933*. As a part of the New Deal, it was a significant change in how business was viewed in Washington. President Roosevelt believed that the root of the problems on Wall Street was a lack of morality. He stated that legislation was required "when evils are not eradicated by people in the business in which the evil exists" (Parrish, 197, p. 43). He had watched many families lose their savings, and he blamed the investment bankers for these tragedies. He demanded much more disclosure and requirements for honesty in the marketing of securities products. This oversight of marketing has become a common practice today. Any marketing piece created must be cleared through compliance before being released to the public. Marketing is to be filed with FINRA, and there are strict requirements for what cannot be said and, more importantly, what must be included. The regulatory oversight of marketing materials and the method of marketing are highly regulated due to the humble beginnings of the request for truth and fairness that Roosevelt initiated.

Roosevelt also expected oversight and supervision of stock exchanges. The Securities Act of 1933 provided powers to the Federal Trade Commission to begin overseeing investment bankers, ensuring that they follow prescribed methods in offering and advertising securities. It is referred to as the *truth in securities law*, and it has two main objectives. First, it requires that investors receive financial and other significant information concerning securities being offered for public sale, and secondly, it prohibits deceit, misrepresentations, and other fraud in the sale of securities (www.sec.gov, retrieved 2010). The Glass-Steagall Act was also implemented at this time. This law required separation between banks and investment firms, and it created the FDIC, providing insurance for bank savings accounts. This was the beginning of the oversight of the securities industry.

As a part of the New Deal, there was broad support to implement these new measures to apply controls to individual investments. The public expected that this would solve the problem. While they had been covered previously by state laws, clearly that had been determined to be inadequate. With different states applying different laws, consumers were not able to develop a thorough understanding of what protections were available to them. Some states still had no laws, and others that had laws did not generally interfere to any large extent. Consequently, regardless of any state laws, most consumers were still considered very much on their own, without regulatory protection. The Securities Act of 1933 should have been the correction of this situation. All consumers would now be covered by one uniform set of laws, regardless of the states. It began modestly, and some were hopeful that it would prevent the type of experience they had just lived through from ever happening again. Even at the beginning, however, there was some skepticism in terms of the ability to change the course of business practices through legislation. Felix Frankfurter, for example, commented, "Business morals must undergo a considerable change for the better to accompany effectively the self-disciplinary portion of the act" (deBedtz, 1964, p. 53). Others were concerned that the bill would have no real power, because the government was so beholden to the business community at this time. Even those who were largely in favor of regulations were concerned that the laws would not be effective.

# CHAPTER 6

# The Birth of Securities Regulation I: The Establishment of the Securities and Exchange Commission

WITH THE CREATION of the Securities Exchange Commission (SEC), all oversight of the securities industry was placed in the hands of this new organization and removed from the Federal Trade Commission. This became known as the *Securities Exchange Act of 1934* and was passed with overwhelming support in both houses of Congress (deBedtz, 1964, p. 75). The goal of the act was to protect the consumer from abuses in the industry and to ensure this ongoing protection by creating an agency to do just that, to prevent the *evil* corporate insiders from benefitting from their knowledge at the expense of other investors. Some practices were outlawed altogether, and reporting processes were implemented, giving the government information about individual companies. Audits were required, and the SEC reserved the right to require additional information if it was not satisfied with the results of the audit.

The new law included a provision that separated out the public functions of a broker from the personal trading of a dealer. The most important piece of the legislation, arguably, was the power it gave the SEC to prevent presumed or alleged corrupt practices and to make changes as it deemed appropriate to serve this goal (deBedtz, 1964, p. 81). By establishing this new government entity and empowering it with the oversight, implementation, correction, and punishment of entities and individuals, the government felt that had solved the problem. President Roosevelt considered this piece of his New Deal to be significant and successful.

During the first few years after the SEC was created, there was a great deal of activity. Efforts were made to encourage significant changes to the securities industry, and the first individuals assigned to run the SEC took their responsibilities very seriously. The business, however, was largely uninterrupted. A great relief to Wall Street was the appointment of Joseph Kennedy as Chairman of the SEC. Kennedy had made a fortune on Wall Street and was not viewed as someone likely to turn his back on his friends. As expected, he continued to be friendly to Wall Street during his years on the SEC. While regulations were created and implemented, the view and perspective of "the Street" was reflected in the Chairman of the SEC himself. The appointment of Kennedy ensured some security for Wall Street, and there was respect for him from all corners.

Some positive actions in the first few years included registration of securities traded on national exchanges, requirements for financial reporting, oversight of exchanges and broker/dealers, anti-fraud provisions, and prohibitions against wash sales. Standards were implemented, and margin credit was now restricted (Phillips, 1981, p. 10). With these adjustments and very minor interference beyond that, most Wall Street insiders considered the SEC to be reasonable and decent. There was very little opposition to the first few new developments because they were not onerous and were not illogical. Then, after those first few years, the SEC became a non-event. The securities industry laws were heralded with the roar of a lion in the 1930s, then subsequently went out like a lamb with the Investment Advisors Act of 1940.

After the fanfare and flurry of activity the first few years, the SEC became largely irrelevant in the 1950s. The only noise in the 1950s was an attempt by the states to make changes to securities law ensuring some uniformity among the states. While this made a few headlines, there was no significant impact on the industry, and the SEC remained in the shadows during this time. Staff was reduced significantly from 1950 to 1955, and it was considered a largely irrelevant organization (Phillips, 1981, p. 13). Many people forgot that the SEC existed, and business continued undisturbed for many years. It was not until the 1970s that the SEC again ramped up its staffing, increased its budget, and began the process of investigating some of the activities on the American Stock Exchange.

## Progress

During the 1970s, after a few irregular reports came to the attention of the SEC, concerns arose about a company trading on the AMEX with questionable financials, potential bribes, and international bribery. Once this situation became public, the SEC was once again in the spotlight. The agency was questioned, and some investors wondered if the SEC was having any impact at all. The SEC defended itself and sought to make itself relevant once again. In spite of the regulations put in place previously, it appeared that business had been continuing as usual, and "usual" was not without some portion of irregularities. When questioned about the value of the organization and the impact of regulatory laws, the Chairman of the SEC, Roderick Hills, advised in May of 1976, "Each proposed new regulation should be examined in the light of available economic evidence before being adopted. Monitoring programs should be created to permit us to determine later whether or not regulations we adopt are producing the results we expect" (Phillips, 1976, p. 1).

## The Excessive 1980S

During the 1980s, a new product arrived on the horizon that became known as *junk bonds*. The name aptly described the product. These bonds were higher risk but also included a higher interest rate. Many men who are now household names made their fortune selling these junk bonds. Ivan Boesky and Mike Milken were two of them.

Milken was rewarded by his firm, Drexel Burnham, for his brilliant strategy of substituting junk bonds for equity. While this certainly brought in a great deal of revenue for the firm, it became evident that something was not right at Drexel Burnham, and eventually the Securities and Exchange Commission stepped in.

After the fall of Milken and the bankruptcy of Drexel Burnham, executives at the firm were questioned about the strategy. They explained that they were able to do anything they wanted, and so they "leveraged themselves and their clients to the hilt without preparing for the day debt would go out of fashion." One former officer commented to a reporter from *Fortune Magazine* in May of 1990, "We thought we were invulnerable" (Galbraith, 1990, p. 97, quoting *Fortune Magazine*, May 21, 1990, pp. 90-96). In the 1980s, other products also provided opportunities for investors to make a great deal of money very quickly, or lose it just as quickly. According to Galbraith, index and option trading added casino effects into the market. While the products were certainly risky, the underlying problem still remained that people bought in without expecting a downturn. Galbraith referred to the continued interest in new products rising to popularity in the securities industry as an erroneous belief on the part of so many individuals in this country that "effortless enrichment is an entitlement" (Galbraith, 1990, p. 97).

## Leverage And Entitlement

More and more, we see the growth of entitlements in this country while the demand just continues relentlessly. There certainly seems to be greed and a perception on behalf of some Americans that they should be given all that they desire without working to achieve it. The American dream has always been based on achievement and opportunity. Learn, study, work hard, and be honest, we are told, and we will be successful. The new *euphoria* is based on getting without merit and withdrawing without ever depositing into the system. This attitude stems from a decaying human factor and results in a resentful society and a bitter community of people. This attitude also results in outlandish expectations that cannot ever be met and, when they are not met, outcomes include complaints, lawsuits, and additional regulations designed to correct whatever egregious wrongs the stock market, Wall Street, or the economy itself allegedly insulted individuals with.

What each period of economic failure seems to have in common is the use of leverage. During the rise up to the crash of 1929 and the Great Depression, the use of margin accounts (i.e., leverage) began in earnest. During the 1980s, leverage was applied excessively in the form of corporate takeovers and leveraged buyouts. Much of this was done with debt financing. According to Galbraith, the crash of 1987 was as predictable as the crash of 1929, and he refers to them both as a "day of reckoning" (Galbraith, 1990, p. 98).

In the early 1990s, Congress began reviewing the securities industry yet again with an eye on compensation of executives. Ironically, they expected this to fix the system by requiring disclosure of all executive salaries and bonuses and details behind the salary structure. The open disclosure was expected to minimize corruption within the industry. In 1993, new legislation required securities firms to provide the SEC with not only the amounts being paid, but also the methodology and process behind the payments and payment decisions.

In October 1996, Congress passed a bill titled the National Securities Markets Improvement Act of 1996 (NSMIA). As this bill became law, it extensively amended various provisions of the Securities Act of 1933, the Securities Exchange Act of 1934, the Trust Indenture Act of 1939, the Investment Company Act of 1940, and the Investment Advisers Act of 1940. This act allowed states to continue to protect themselves against fraud in the securities market, but it clarified the relationship between federal and state regulators. This represented the first major change in legislation since the New Deal, and many considered it a badly needed update to existing laws (www.sifma.org, 11/1/2010).

With this law, Congress established a hierarchy and more firmly developed a bureaucratic structure of regulatory authority, but many thought the improved organization helped to make federal regulations more logical and efficient. Some welcomed the changes made through the National Securities Markets Improvements Act as it attempted to clarify situations where state law and federal law seemed to contradict one another. However, it also essentially put the SEC and the federal government first in line for any oversight and for enforcement of any requirements. NSMIA "preempts state registration and related requirements in the case of nationally traded securities and securities of registered investment companies" (SIFMA.org, 11/1/2010). The provision regarding broker/dealers was beneficial to the organizations responsible for reporting to the SEC. The law placed the lead authority for record-keeping requirements with the SEC as opposed to the states. This prevented multi-state reporting requirements for those who conducted business in more than one state, but it also made the SEC more powerful and allowed the federal government to be more intrusive.

It may be noted that, during this time in Congress, the mid-term elections stunned the country, as many Democrat seats turned over into Republican hands. The election of 1996 brought the Contract with America and the Gingrich Revolution. Politically, this election represented a strong desire in the country to return to the years when Americans felt that their freedoms were secure and their values protected. It would have been very appropriate and highly logical that during this time in our country's political history the securities industry would try to minimize the impact of regulation, and the intent of NSMIA seems to be just that. Hierarchical organization would imply more efficiency and minimize duplication between the federal government and various state laws. Consistent with the Contract with America and the vision of a capitalist, free market economy, the Republican Congress sought to roll back the government intervention of the early 1990s, reducing the regulatory burden on the business community and encouraging growth in the economy.

## The Gramm-Leach-Bliley Financial Modernization Act of, 1999

One piece of legislation, heavily supported by the Clinton administration, was passed just under the wire as a Republican was about to take the White House in 2000. The Gramm-Leach-Bliley Financial Modernization Act of 1999 was passed very anticlimactically. Primarily, it reversed a good portion of the Glass-Steagall Act and allowed banks and investment companies to be able to work together. The concept behind this act was a type of diversification, allowing investors to benefit from bull markets while defending against bear markets, with the ability to have partial assets with a savings account and partial assets with an investment account. With this act, investors would be able to do both savings and investment at the same financial institution (www.banking.senate.gov, 12/1/2010).

Many firms had already been functioning in this capacity, and the change in the law only gave them the legal green light to continue doing business as they intended. Few objectors noted that the possibility existed for mergers and *too big to fail* institutions. These objections were quickly overlooked, as the bill passed easily. Interestingly, one of the main proponents of this bill was the CEO of Citibank, who purchased Travelers Insurance and created CitiCorp, a bank, investment firm, and insurance company all in one. The full range of financial products available now at CitiCorp would have been illegal under Glass-Steagall. Under the Gramm-Leach-Bliley Act, this was now an accepted practice: "Money is the measure of capitalist achievement; the more money, the greater the achievement and the intelligence that supports it" (Galbraith, 1990, p. 14). Although it had been illegal, the behemoth CitiCorp deemed that it be allowed; therefore the law was changed to accommodate their business growth plan.

Much of the process of developing the new law smelled a little funny. While CitiCorp acquired Travelers and changed its business structure prior to the change in the law, it seemed nonetheless completely confident that it would be standing in the right place, and it was Congress that would take the steps forward to accommodate Citi, rather than Citi accommodating the law. Again, we have to consider the motivation of members of Congress, who are supposed to be conducting the people's business. Is this direction a sign of continued deterioration of the human factor, or is it just a case of one highly motivated, profit-driven CEO at CitiCorp?

It should be noted that during the drafting of the legislation, several top Citigroup officials were included in the process. While Congress debated the bill, one of its strong proponents was Robert Rubin, who was the treasury secretary under President Bill Clinton from 1995 to 1999 (U.S. Treasury Department). Once the bill was signed into law, Rubin left the Treasury department to join CitiCorp, accepting what one could only assume to be a very lucrative position. In 1999, he became the director of Citigroup Finance Canada, one of three top leadership slots within CitiCorp (investing.businessweek. com). Was he really the best person for this job, or was it a reward for assurance of his powerful support of Gramm-Leach-Bliley?

Additional components of the Gramm-Leach-Bliley legislation provided privacy and safeguards for the public. GLBA required that firms notify each of their investors of the privacy requirements at the time they open an account, and then they must mail a new privacy notice once a year for each subsequent year the relationship stays in place. The notice allows consumers to opt out of any communication, saving themselves from further marketing and advertising. The safeguards rule was also a privacy protection provision. It was designed to provide consumers with an understanding of how the firm would protect non-public information, such as account balances and types of accounts. Each firm was required to develop a written security plan if it did not already have one in place, and this plan would place responsibility for implementation squarely on the shoulders of named individuals. Ideally, this part of the law was to ensure that firms were developing the systems and securing the data they maintained from their clients. The bill made IT professionals responsible for not only systems, but also the security and privacy of systems.

It could be argued that several pieces of the Gramm-Leach-Bliley Act were designed to protect consumers. Allowing customers to invest, save, and purchase insurance within one company made a great deal of sense to a great many people. It allowed for convenience for the customer and efficiency for the company. The privacy protections were certainly a well-intentioned attempt to maintain customer confidentiality. The reality, however, was that many of the firms that became diversified in their business also became *too big to fail*. It is certainly noteworthy that the company that led the charge to be allowed to grow well beyond its banking roots into the unchartered territory of investment and the big business of insurance was the same company that became the personification of *too big to fail* and one of the largest recipients of TARP money in 2009. CitiBank bought Smith Barney, an investment firm, and became CitiGroup. CitiGroup bought Travelers Insurance and became CitiCorp. After fewer than 10 years and with loss after loss and a huge government bailout, Citi looks like it may be *too big NOT to fail*.

One of the other unintended consequences of a well-intentioned bill was the burden the privacy requirements placed on small firms. Large corporations could afford a mass mailing and annual mailings with a minor adjustment to the budget. For small firms, it was a major impact on the budget that eliminated many other previously planned activities. It also required a significant amount of labor and time that most small firms do not have readily available. Staff members normally assigned to other priorities were taken out of their regular jobs for weeks at a time to accomplish the enormous requirements for privacy. In some cases, just implementing the safeguarding plan and upgrading technology was a burden. All of these requirements, though seemingly innocuous, were in fact deadly to some of the very small firms. The long-term consequence of so many smaller companies exiting the playing field is the continued growth of only the very large firms and the perpetuation of the *too big to fail* businesses, which have become the bailout brigade.

## Sarbanes-Oxley (Sox) Act of 2002

The names of Kenneth Lay and Jeff Skilling are well known now. They were the two primary villains in the part of recent history that began with the explosion of Enron and ended with the implementation of Sarbanes-Oxley (SOX). Enron began to unwind in the late

1990s but remained afloat until the house came tumbling down in 2002, taking all of its employees, their pensions, and stockholder investments with them. The employees lost, not just their jobs and current source of income, but also their retirement in the form of future income invested in Enron stock. While there were many other companies exposed during this time, Enron has to be the personification of greed and financial fraud and corruption.

During many accounting meetings throughout 1999 and 2001, the auditors from Arthur Anderson warned the Enron board of directors that Enron's accounting practices were considered *high risk* (Byrne, 2002, pp. 50-51). The audit committee on the board was told that Enron was pushing limits and that they were functioning "at the edge of what was considered acceptable accounting practices" (Byrne, 2002, pp. 50-51). In spite of these warnings, not one member of the board of directors asked for more information or suggested looking into these issues more thoroughly. It was clear after the investigation revealed what was going on behind closed doors that if the board had taken its responsibility seriously and if it had asked questions and investigated Arthur Anderson's concerns, the implosion of Enron could have been prevented.

Some of what was discovered after the implosion seems almost impossible to have gone unrecognized. For example, it was revealed that Ken Lay had his own personal credit line at Enron that eventually reached $7.5 million. Although this was cash taken out of the company, he was allowed to repay the loan with stock (Byrne, John, Business Week, 2002, pp. 50-51). This became his primary method of dumping his Enron stock when he knew it was going to become worthless. He ultimately extracted $77 million in cash from the company, which was replaced with the worthless stock. In addition to this incredible misuse of company funds, the board also approved levels of compensation that defy logic. During 2000, when the total net income from the company was $975 million, the board approved compensation in the amount of $750 million. Approximately two-thirds of the company revenues were going out the door in employee compensation. The board should not have approved that, quite clearly. The board also should have been concerned about the debt, which was farmed out to Merrill Lynch, consequently dragging them into the abyss along with Enron. The board should have been looking toward shareholder value and investment in the future of the company, not just lining the pockets of its friends.

Unfortunately, prior to Ken Lay's rape and pillage of Enron, although the board's ignorance is astounding, there was no legal avenue to hold them accountable. A lack of ethics was obvious, but a legal remedy was elusive. It was initially even difficult to hold Ken Lay responsible, as he feigned a lack of knowledge and attempted to shift the accountability to the CFO. Although a moral compass or any sense of integrity would have prevented the Enron explosion, it was determined that it must take a series of new laws to prevent this from happening again. No one considered the consequence of severe human factor decay and its ongoing deterioration that was evident in many corporate corners and in society as a whole. Instead of considering the severe human factor and the implications of its astronomical deterioration, the solution offered to corporate corruption was once again a legal solution, which became the Sarbanes-Oxley Act of 2002.

Regulations under Sarbanes-Oxley included a new public company oversight accounting board reporting under the SEC. This new board expands the authority of the SEC deeper into accounting processes. The law made the audit committee of the board responsible for the financials, and it required all financials to be signed by both the CFO and CEO. The CEO and CFO certification of financial reports included all financial reports and even off-balance sheet transactions. No CEO would be able to claim a lack of awareness, thinking they are excused by just blaming the CFO. The CEO was put squarely in the hot seat under Sarbanes-Oxley (Miller, & Pushkoff, 2002). The law also tightened up retention requirements. This was in response to several scandals that involved the shredding of documents. Companies could not shred, but rather had to save so that damaging documents

46

could be found. An unintended consequence of this provision, again, disproportionately impacted smaller companies. The requirement to retain paperwork resulted in a need for more office space, not for employees, but for files. For some small companies, this added more overhead costs to their budget just to fulfill this requirement. Ironically, it is usually large companies that cause the problems, but small companies that bear the cross of the added regulatory outcomes.

Sarbanes-Oxley also added a whistleblower provision. It encouraged employees to come forward, and it provided protection for them when they were reporting fraud. There was a whistleblower at Enron, and she was largely responsible for bringing attention to the accounting irregularities and problems with the firm. The SEC explained that these reforms were designed to encourage corporate responsibility and to combat corporate and accounting fraud (Miller & Pushkoff, 2002). The entire bill was very responsive to the crisis and had the intention of preventing another Enron, but it had a different effect. Whether it stopped any accounting fraud is certainly questionable, but what is undeniable is the financial impact to the bottom line of small companies in America. The reporting requirements were onerous, and many companies had to increase the cost of their technology significantly just to accommodate the law. According to some IT professionals, the budget impact to their departments made almost any other activity impossible. Compliance with SOX was a costly process.

Scandal after scandal seemed to plague the country in the early turn of the century. From Enron to WorldCom to Tyco, companies were being exposed and fraudulent practices revealed. The Sarbanes-Oxley Act of 2002 was a response to all of these corporate failures. The law put tighter reporting requirements on companies and held both the CEO and CFO responsible for financial reporting. The new law set standards for financial reporting and required a signature on audited financials from both the company CEO as well as the chief financial officer. This specific requirement covered the excuse that the Enron CEO, Kenneth Lay, gave which was essentially the ridiculously unbelievable "I didn't know."

# CHAPTER 7

# The Birth of Securities Regulation II: Shackling Wall Street in the Chains of Government

THE CURRENT CLIMATE is, once again, anti-Wall Street, and as we wait for the implementation of the next phase of regulations, one cannot help but wonder what difference it will make. Wall Street has become a scapegoat for the poor economic situation the country is in. With continued high unemployment, ongoing foreclosures, and investments dropping for many Americans, the White House needs to point the finger of blame away from Washington, D.C. Wall Street makes for a likely villain. After seeing the huge salaries, excessive bonuses, and lavish parties, it is easy for struggling Americans to join *the lynch mob mentality of stringing up* Wall Street CEOs and congratulating Congress for going after the gluttons with gusto. They applaud the efforts and cheer the new regulations as retribution and deserved punishment. The more chains the federal government shackles to Wall Street players, the more satisfied jilted investors become.

However, while it may satisfy the anger of the mob mentality, it will not change any future activities. In spite of the growth of the SEC, the organization established entirely to ensure legal compliance and regulatory oversight, it did not catch any of the recent crisis or crimes on Wall Street. Bernie Madoff made millions without being challenged. Goldman Sachs just paid a fine for practices that went on under the nose of SEC and FINRA regulators for years. Lehman Brothers lost millions and went out of business. American International Group (AIG), CitiCorp, Bank of America, and others jumped on the public dole when their practices led to the worst recession in recent history. Where was the SEC? Where was FINRA? According to recent news reports, many of the highly paid bureaucrats charged with the responsibility of oversight of the securities industry spent much of their time on their computers looking at pornography. President Roosevelt is surely spinning in his grave.

Regulations implemented during Roosevelt's presidency should have protected the public, and yet they did not. The reliance on laws and a legal system to control human behavior is problematic, and our belief that the solution to a decaying human factor is additional laws is flawed. As long as there are laws, there are ways to avoid them. Creativity and intelligence are not in short supply in this society. With ambition, fueled by greed, there will always be those willing to violate the laws or find loopholes in the laws to achieve their goals of wealth and power. Individuals with free will make choices, and it is the decisions that each person makes that determine the course of their actions. Those with a healthy human factor will use judgment constructed with integrity, morality, and a sense of responsibility. The decaying human factor would drive behaviors of dishonesty and recklessness, with a lack of concern for the well-being of others. No number of laws, rules, or regulations can change the impact of a decaying human factor.

The regulatory changes proposed by Congress and signed by President Obama in July 2010 are now hailed as the most significant changes in regulatory law since *the Securities Acts of 1933 and 1934*. Will Frank-Dodd make a difference? One thing is clearly evident: The federal government has found an excuse to create yet another bureaucracy. While the SEC could not find fraud and FINRA did not notice violations, these organizations will continue to do the job they clearly could not do while another agency is added for identical purposes. When Americans realized the post office was not reliable, we turned to private companies such as FedEx and UPS. We certainly did not expect that a second or a third post office would be any better than the first one.

Current opinions vary on the status of the securities industry and the benefits and liabilities of the federal regulations that pertain to the industry. As we entered the recessionary period beginning in 2007, the responses were quick, aggressive, and of a yet-to-be-determined value. During the recent economic crisis, the blaming and accusing was very typical and consistent with previous patterns of behaviors. Starting with the events leading up to the crisis, we can draw significant parallels to the experience of the Great Depression and the stock market crash of 1929. As reviewed in Chapter 1, new entrants to the stock market and a system with a great deal of leverage preempted the crash. People bought on margin and began using debt in record amounts. When the bill came due for outstanding debts, the dominoes began falling. In 2007, similar circumstances existed. Prosperous years led many people to believe that the stock market could only go up, and the mood was largely very optimistic about investments.

The beginning of the current crisis can be traced to the debt specifically in the mortgage industry. Just like the stock market, people had the expectation that the value of property would only continue to rise. Property values had indeed increased over the vast majority of years, but there is more than one direction that the values can move, and in 2007, they moved what most Americans considered to be in the very wrong direction. Home values plummeted, taking families down with them. Many could no longer afford mortgages that were made available through either weak or fraudulent loans, and adjustable rate mortgage rates caught many unprepared.

The failure of large banks and the infusion of capital required for firms such as AIG were largely tied to the derivatives market and their purchase of mortgage-backed securities through the derivatives market. Because derivatives were unregulated, it was much easier for companies to make these types of investments. People and companies that invested in these products were unaware of the low quality of these investments. Even relying on ratings was pointless in this case, as the ratings did not accurately convey the poor content of the products. Through a combination of problems, errors, and fraudulent behavior, the extensive amount of rancid mortgages were thrust into the economy, ready to explode at any time.

Explosion is exactly what happened to the economy toward the end of 2007. Again, eerily similar to the 1930s, Americans had excessive debt and little concern for consequences. Many owned homes they could barely afford and even added to their burden of debt by taking second and third mortgages or lines of credit from their perceived strength of investment, the home. As the lessons of the Great Depression should have taught us, enjoying the prosperous times is fine as long as we are prepared for the inevitable rainy day. When it rained in 1939, Americans got soaked. When it rained in 2007, many went for a swim. As home values decreased, many could not even sell to get out from debt. A large number of Americans quickly found that they were upside down on payments, owing much more than the value of their home was worth. Foreclosures began and have continued steadily in record numbers.

The corporate fall-out was similar. American companies also participated in the gluttony of debt, investing heavily in high-risk products and risky mortgages or mortgage-backed securities products. In addition to the debt crisis, a parallel crisis of character ingratiated itself into the corporate leadership. Barely beyond the shadow of Enron, Tyco, and Worldcom, we have AIG, Lehman Brothers and Bernie Madoff. While Lehman failed taking jobs and investor confidence with it, AIG hung on thanks to the American taxpayer bailout. Making congressional pork look paltry, AIG used the taxpayer-provided bailout to fund conferences at exotic locations and excessive bonuses to executives. The American taxpayer felt abused, abandoned, and defrauded once again.

The new legislation will involve more oversight. We have had oversight since the 1930s. The new legislation will include derivatives, which it did not do in the past. This is the pattern. Add a new product and find a new loophole. Make millions. Avoid the cameras when you are caught and retire to a life of luxury, leaving others holding the bag. Those who were frauded, jilted, or abandoned demand action. Congress adopts laws; regulatory authorities implement them. Perpetrators find new products that have not yet been regulated and new loopholes that have not yet been exploited. Does anyone think additional laws will prevent a new product from coming on to the market with the same high-risk strategies that have been brought to the market in the past with so much profit readily available?

The new legislation also addresses 12b-1 fees. Congress, based on its very limited practical knowledge of the industry, determined that the 12b-1 fees were not appropriate, as some brokers were continuing to collect the fees while not serving the clients. There is some reality in the concept that some financial advisors do not do an adequate job, continuing to service clients after the initial commission is received. But if you take away their only ongoing source of revenue from that client, is it likely to increase the amount of service the client receives? Of course it does not. Elimination of the 12b-1 fees dis-incentivizes brokers from providing any service at all. There is no longer an upside, and the downside is significant. One misspoken word or one misinterpreted recommendation, and a broker can find himself or herself in arbitration. The other reality is that many financial advisors have a long list of loyal clients whom they serve dutifully for many years without earning more than the 12b-1 fees, which are usually very small amounts. The amount of service work that dedicated advisors provide to their long-term clients is not compensated anywhere near the level of most highly skilled, qualified professionals. To take away the 12b-1 fees is to tell many hardworking financial advisors that service to their clients is worthless. Not only is it illogical, it is insulting.

# Real Reform

The federal government can continue to add regulations and impose many more laws. With an overview of history since the late 1930s, it is safe to say that no matter how many regulations they add, there is no change. Some Congressmen and women are overly preoccupied with the need to feel useful and justify their existence. Any corporate scandal or crisis presents an opportunity for them. Many of them are not truly interested in solving a problem. At best, their sole interest is in gaining exposure and limelight, grandstanding their shock and amazement at yet another Wall Street disaster. It gives them an opportunity to look like heroes when another villain is uncovered. Congress has become an oligarchy, and many of the occupants of the House and the Senate live so far outside of the realities of middle-class America that even if they wanted to, they would be less likely to understand and then implement a real solution. The people running the government are suffering as much from the decaying human factor as anyone. There is no salvation in more government solutions. At best, it provides a challenge to anyone wanting to circumvent the law, but at worst, it places ethical people in a position of having to invest more time and resources complying with laws that they would never have violated anyway. The impact on private-sector businesses is that some simply cannot afford to remain in business. They find it difficult to comply with all of the laws and stay profitable. Small businesses, in 2012, are under attack and losing the battle rapidly.

As the private sector has been suffering job losses and income reductions, the size of the government continues to grow. Jobs in government now pay more than equal-level jobs in the private sector. Add to the salary the extensive benefits packages and the pension plans, and it is no mystery why this country is drowning in debt. The productive in society are punished while the public employees and unions gouge taxpayers for generous salaries, amazing perks, top-notch benefits, and rich pension plans that private-sector employees can only dream about. Small companies cannot compete with the public sector, and since the recession that began at the end of 2007, many companies have simply given up. They cannot compete with the salaries, cannot afford to hire more employees, and cannot keep up with compliance costs.

As yet another large bill has passed and companies need to shift operations to accommodate the requirements, we can be sure that in another five or 10 years we will encounter an Enron, a Madoff, or an AIG. The problem of poor management and fraudulent practices will not be corrected by government mandates. Regulatory reform has been tried many times and in several different sectors, and yet we continue to have crises and failures. It is time to look for a new solution and one that will actually attack the root cause and solve the problem in a permanent way. The true implication of these results is that the legal solution is nothing more than a quick fix. It deters people from doing one thing but guides them into whatever new areas have not been addressed through the law. As we saw with the recent mortgage-backed securities crisis, one easy way around existing laws is to use a product that has not yet been regulated.

A human factor–based education is the best method to approach the perpetual problems of the securities industry and financial sector. The people employed in this industry need to be changed deeply, in their minds, hearts, and spirits. They need to realize that actions are wrong whether they are caught or not. Regulatory changes just offer unethical people opportunities. They enjoy the challenge and take pride in evading the law. There is always a loophole, always a new method; a more creative way to make money fraudulently. As long as there are people with deteriorating human factor qualities, there will continue to be financial scandals, crises, and diverse forms of corruption in the securities industry.

It is time to look for a better way to address ongoing corruption. Regulations do not work in the presence of severe human factor decay. At best, they put obstacles in the way of good people trying to do an honest job, and they are just minor speed bumps for those intent on criminal or unethical behavior. Instead of regulatory and legal applications that have not worked since the 1930s, it would have been much more beneficial if we had implemented human factor–based education programs. Based on research provided in the following chapter, we present empirical evidence that supports the thesis that additional regulations will not change fraudulent behavior in the American as well as the global marketplace, and only genuinely addressing the issues of human factor decay will have the intended and desired impact.

# CHAPTER 8

# Mandated Government Training Programs: The Quest for a Solution to Moral Failure

AFTER HAVING GATHERED and tabulated results from a survey along with interviews regarding issues of ethics, we were able to develop a picture from both industry insiders and outsiders. Interviews were conducted with several seasoned professionals in the securities industry from sales, compliance, and management. A survey was conducted that was open to everyone, although the majority of respondents was within the industry. For the survey, a series of statements were provided and respondents were asked to choose from the following: strongly agree, agree, no opinion, disagree, or strongly disagree. During the course of researching this issue, many people were also interviewed. Included are some direct quotes from those interviewed in the various Case Studies in addition to survey results. Each interviewee was given a pseudonym so they will remain anonymous.

Regarding business ethics, 81% of respondents in the survey stated that government-mandated training will not stop people from participating in unethical behaviors. Most of the major scandals in the last decade have resulted from the scheming of greedy people. It was not a lack of training. It was a lack of personal commitment to engage in ethical living. If, according to our respondents, government mandated training will not stop people from engaging in unethical behaviors, why is training such a huge component in the securities industry? If training will not stop people from participating in unethical behaviors, what will? To investigate the question, one of the main hypotheses employed is that human factor–based education will change behaviors in such a way that people will make moral/ethical choices in the long term. The superficial values and monetary greed will be minimized. It is those behaviors, motivations, and values that drive people to participate in unethical practices. Money spent on ethics training is money wasted. Money spent on rote response training that does not effect change in the human factor qualities of the individual is a wasted resource.

While taxpayer dollars are spent subsidizing training, people become more creative and energized in finding ways to make more money by going around the law. Financial advisors are always faced with decisions about how to handle clients and their investments. Many of those interviewed felt that it is common sense and their desire to do the right thing for the client that drives them. They will make decisions in the best interest of their clients and do not feel they need Big Brother Regulator looking over their shoulders.

Not only is taxpayer-funded training a waste of taxpayer money, it also results in a waste of time for those participating. If most people are guided by their own principle-centered moral compass, then their path is already established. We can reliably predict how people will behave in the future based on how they have behaved in the past. Those who reliably do a good job, take good care of their clients, and try their best to follow laws, rules, and regulations will continue to do so. Those who are more interested in greed, wealth, and the opportunity to earn a quick dollar no matter what it takes to get there will continue to perform as usual. They can be counted on to ignore laws, violate rules, and justify their lack of ethics. The issue is described by one of the respondents in one of our Case Studies. Referred to as Ben

Pool in Case Study 1B: "Bad brokers are definitely out there. There are some that are completely unethical and do fraudulent things."

## Playing the Game

Regardless of the amount of training, it really comes down to ethical decision-making when financial advisors decide how to respond. In Case Study 1D, Dan Walsh calls it a game:

> It's basically just playing a game and you have to follow the rules of the game. Play the game well and you will do okay, but the game is complicated. The condition of the player is important, the knowledge, techniques. You can be profitable, but compliance is like the referee, and there will always be costs in terms of real dollars and clients. If you can't do something for your client, they will just go elsewhere until they find someone who will do what they ask.

If it is a game, then anyone can learn the rules and play. It then becomes an ethical decision if you implement the rules, abide by the rules, or spend your energy circumventing the rules. You also are faced with situations where the rules may or may not benefit your client and the rules may or may not make sense. If you are guided by moral principles, the rules are irrelevant. Financial advisors driven by their own principle-centered moral compasses do not wait for Congress to tell them how to behave. Frank Laden provides an example of this:

> We had people who wanted to take loans out on their homes to invest. It's always been my policy to turn those people away. Now FINRA does not allow this kind of thing, and clients have to disclose the source of their funds. For some it's too late. They found brokers willing to do this—take a loan and invest it in stocks. People can really lose on something like that. Before it was against the regulations, some of us would never do it anyway. For me, it just never made sense. I

had people insist and I would tell them I would not do it. To refinance your house to buy stocks tells me your expectations are out of line. They think the stock market will keep going up. But what if it goes down?

Those guided by greed and driven by their own self-interests will always find ways around the law. Those who are rich in the positive qualities of the human factor will make the right decisions regardless of the law.

Frank Laden also noted that clients will find someone willing to do what he will not do. For those interested in taking a loan on their house to buy stocks, they would find a financial advisor who would make that investment. Prior to it becoming illegal, there would be only a sense of ethics or healthy human factor that would prevent a financial advisor from handling the transaction, thus earning commission. Frank Laden and others who turn away that business do so to their own detriment. They lose the potential commission. They do so, however, because they believe it is the wrong thing to do.

Consequently, there is no way the law can be responsible for protecting consumers from bad financial advisors or shady broker/dealers. There will always be people intent on doing things that are harmful if they are driven by their own self-interests and greed. Frank Laden describes the greed of management and the role it plays in a broker/dealer: "That's why bad business is allowed to happen—because upper management browbeats lower-level compliance with the threat of losing their job."

The role of management is also examined in our survey. One statement in the survey asserts that: "The real problem in the brokerage industry lies with greedy management." A total of 45% agree, while only 26% disagree. With 25% not choosing to agree or disagree with this statement, those who are aware of the role of management are strongly in support of the statement. Some respondents simply do not know how to respond to this statement because they are either not involved in the industry or not involved at a high-enough level to be aware of what upper management is doing. Regardless of the amount, level, or expense of training, the true problem of unethical behavior will persist. A decaying human factor guarantees a population impacted by a strong flare for acts of fraud.

When asked about what the biggest problems were in the industry, Dan Walsh stated: "We need a code of ethics. The bottom line is what is being looked at the big banks. Have they been ethical? From the top down, they were not ethical. My opinion of those entities is pretty poor." If regulators are busy looking at everyone, they are limited in their time, and most regulators are compelled to complete their review within a timely manner. They are under pressure. It is not hard to understand why so many of the major players escape justice while the minor players are completely at the mercy of regulators. The small broker/dealers are frustrated, exhausted, and gasping for the breath or survival. Rather than spending money on taxpayer-funded training, real ethics should be the goal. That requires reaching a person's soul, not just their ears.

## Management: Influence and Excessive Compensation

A total of 78% of respondents supported the statement that poor management has caused more problems in the brokerage industry than financial advisors. If this is true, then that is another reason training financial advisors is useless. Most top-level managers do not participate in training. If they do have to sit through the ethics course or anything else, it is usually done on a computer, in the middle of a hectic day and with little attention paid to the information. Even if they do pay attention, is it less likely to matter to a greedy CEO on the verge of collecting a multi-million dollar bonus? There have been few cases in history when a big Wall Street firm walked away from a multi-million dollar bonus due to ethical reasons. The few firms that avoided the mortgage-backed securities, however, refused to become involved in a high-risk product that could lose as quickly as it could gain.

Many firms that lost a great deal of money during the downturn, borrowing from the U.S. government, still paid their top managers huge bonuses. These people have an entitlement mentality, and it does not matter to them how they perform. They believe they deserve their salary regardless of how poorly their company is doing. While certain companies literally fight for survival, top executives fly in private jets and vacation in luxurious overseas locations. There have certainly been cases where management was directly the cause of a problem in a securities firm. The taxpayer is left footing the bill, and the employees lose their source of income while the executives sob all the way to the bank. AIG, for example, shortly after receiving taxpayer bailout money, intended to move forward with an elaborate sales retreat, until exposed by the media. They also used bailout money to pay excessive bonuses to employees. Many of those provided with government handouts still gave out big bonuses. In a year when many Americans lost their jobs and some even lost their homes, to see hard-earned tax dollars being handed out to leaders at failed institutions was disheartening, perhaps appalling.

## Government Training: The Costs and Consequences

The topic of training provides some interesting results. We observed in the survey that a high percentage of people think that government-mandated training programs provided have some value. It is almost completely equal in the three categories. A total of 36% agree with this statement: Government-mandated education and employee training is a good use of taxpayer dollars. Nearly the same number, 31%, disagree with that statement. Yet another 30% neither agree nor disagree. The same statement is worded slightly differently and yet the same results occur. Statement 24: "Education and training provided by the federal government is largely a waste of resources." Again we see the split between three categories equally. While this statement is more aggressive, it still garners 28% agreement. While 34% disagree with the statement, 30% neither agree nor disagree. If we only look at those choosing a clear position, we could infer that half of the respondents believe that mandatory training provided by the government is a waste of resources.

As we take it a step further, we consider the responses of those who think government training has some benefit. Even though 36% stated that government-mandated training is a good use of taxpayer dollars, they also acknowledge that training, as it is, will not improve the ethical behavior of most people. The statement: Training will stop people from participating in unethical behaviors) garners only 4% support. A total of 82% disagree with that statement. In a similar statement, 67% disagree: "Financial training developed by the government transforms our population into principle-centered people." Only 2% agreed with that statement. Another concerning response was to the following statement: "Ongoing government training programs have transformed me into a person who will do the right thing for a client." Only 8% agree with that statement.

The comments of the respondents in the training area indicate a desire for training and an appreciation for any support of the goal to do an excellent job. According to several of the respondents in the case studies, individual brokers know that they need to be provided with regular updates and guidance in order to stay within the regulations. They expressed frustration when regulations change often and they know they need to keep up. They explained how seriously they take their commitment to the regulatory environment and their interest in doing things exactly according to the law, even if they think the law is nonsensical. It is in their best interest to follow compliance as closely as possible. Al First describes his interest in ongoing government-mandadted training programs with the following comments:

> I insist on keeping up to date on compliance because there is no way around it. It is here to stay. I try to encourage the broker/dealer to stay on top of it and keep me informed of compliance issues. [Compliance] is necessary to protect the public and to keep reps and broker/dealers in line. I expect the compliance staff to do their job and keep informed of changes in the regulatory environment so I can do my job with the people.

Brokers interviewed also expressed frustration with the vagueness of the training and regulatory updates they are provided. The regulatory agencies offer vague guidelines, leaving much up to interpretation. It becomes a game of gotcha in some cases, or at least some brokers feel that way, as they cannot be exactly sure what a rule might say, but they can get caught doing something they did not know was wrong. The data gathered in the survey support that theory. Brokers want more training, not less. They want better information and clearer guidance. They want to follow the rules but just need clarity on what they are.

Training, as most agree and the data support, will not change the ethical nature of those intent on behaving in a fraudulent manner. The data indicate that 81% of the respondents believe that training will not stop people from participating in unethical behaviors. Brokers who are already functioning in an ethical manner crave more direction from regulators because the regulators decide the rules of the game regardless of ethical principles. A broker who would normally rely on his own moral compass or business principles can no longer do so because he has to respond to government bureaucrats and comply with manmade laws often coming from those unfamiliar with the business; or quite possibly any business. Those who have intent to defraud have the regulations from FINRA, SEC, and various other bureaucrats to use as a road map to find the easiest loopholes.

## Held Hostage by Unions

Thanks to an education system held hostage by the teachers union, regardless of the awareness, we are helpless to stop the transition into becoming a nation of greedy, arrogant individuals instead of a community of selfless people who are service-oriented in terms of principle-centeredness. The teachers union is a perfect example of how greed and selfishness have destroyed a very important segment of society. Teachers unions long ago abandoned any interest in education in their pursuit of self-glorification and enrichment. Never has a bigger fraud been played out on the American people, with the public relations machine of teachers unions convincing everyone that teachers are underpaid and yet overworked public servants. They are, in many locations, well compensated and richly compensated in terms of benefits and retirement programs. Generally, they work fewer hours than most other types of employees, and those who feel teaching is their calling should be insulted at the shrillness of the complaints from the industry participants. Those gifted to teach do it because they love it. They are good at it and, consequently, they have the ability to impact the lives of many students over a long career. Gifted and talented teachers would most likely be drawn to their calling regardless of the difference on co-pay on their medical visits. These teachers are about the business of teaching. Teachers unions have made teaching about the business of labor unions.

People largely stated that they thought training was important, yet when they are asked if government-mandated training is a good use of taxpayer dollars, only 36% said that it was. Almost an equal amount, 31%, thought it was not a good use of taxpayer dollars. The respondents believe training is important and that there are better ways to provide it than through government mandates and resources. They are aware that anything done by the government is less effective and more costly than a comparable product produced in the private sector. Another statement from the survey: "I am motivated to acquire more knowledge about my business regardless of government mandates." A total of 89% agree with this statement. Because 89% of respondents are motivated to acquire more knowledge, it is likely that they are willing to find training regardless of whether the government is mandating training. This is further evidence in support of the hypothesis that training programs offered by the government do not result in significant change. But tax dollars are spent regardless of the outcome. Those with the right attitude are willing do what it takes, and they feel responsible for their own training. They are going to attend training, improve their skills, and take ownership for their own development. They want to be better so they can do a better job for their clients. When training is mandatory, it takes ownership from the individual and envelopes it within the state.

Most mandatory training programs are developed with taxpayer dollars or at least subsidized with taxpayer dollars, and then often the firm will pick up the balance of the expense. Those outside the industry are probably largely unaware that their taxpayer dollars are supporting mandatory training that, while some deem it helpful, clearly will never solve the problem in the brokerage industry, because the problem involves moral capital and spiritual capital, and the industry training provides only knowledge and skills, or human capital.

## Who Really Runs the Wild West?

The respondents indicated they are not willing to have no oversight at all, given that there are some brokers who are ethically challenged and, given the percentage of people blaming management, securities industry management is an issue. It is interesting to observe that a higher percentage of the respondents seemed to view management as guilty of ethical lapses rather than individual brokers. In the securities industry, there is a great deal of scrutiny of individual brokers and daily transactions which may be highly ineffective if the ethical lapses come from upper management.

In Case Study 1F, Frank Laden comments on the irony of non-licensed people managing licensed people. The licensed people have all the risk, while the unlicensed people have none. Compliance staff report up the chain of command, and if they find a violation of regulations, they can be prevented from stopping the activity by a greedy CEO who believes the profits justify the risk. While the OSJ or compliance officer could lose his job or license and consequently his or her ability to earn a living, non-licensed management has little at risk. Laden explains it this way:

> OSJs at some of these firms allow it to happen because unlicensed management convinces them to let it go because the management wants to bring in the revenue. The OSJs get

pressured to bring in more revenue, so they are pressured to let trades go through. Once management gets on them, OSJs just shrivel up and go away. These non-FINRA regulated managers have no risk, but they get all the reward if they are earning money based on the investment program income. They are getting bonuses for what brokers do. That's why bad business is allowed to happen, because upper management browbeats lower-level compliance and OSJs with the threat of losing their jobs.

## Moral Issues

There is no other industry that is governed, managed, and reviewed so closely. No other industry comes with the huge investment of oversight and all the government bureaucracy that goes along with that. While the expenses for government have continued to grow, the size of the scandals has as well. People who cite the concern for the need for oversight may consider that the responsibility of financial advisors is significant. People's entire retirement and ability to live independently into their golden years depends on a good financial plan and retirement program. A good financial advisor is one key to the success of any retirement program and can have detrimental effects if decisions are not made with the best information. Is this a unique relationship, however, between a client and a service provider? Are there no other groups of people who have the same high level of responsibility? How about doctors? There we are talking about actual life and death. How about automobile makers? Could they also have accountability for life and death? Think of all of the recalls. What about those who invest in a business or, for example, in a franchise?

## Unethical Practices: Is the Securities Industry Alone?

Doctors use the best available knowledge and resources, and all of their experiences and skills, to diagnose a medical problem and find a solution. Are they expected to consult with a government bureaucrat before initiating a procedure with a patient? At this point, no, although under *Obamacare*, that may be coming. Right now, they do not have a medical compliance staff on site to review every decision, and they never report to any government officials, nor do they have a government entity come in and audit at will. If there is a problem with a particular doctor, there are government entities that may become involved, and the licensing board can revoke a license. But the assumption on a daily basis is that doctors can be trusted to do the job they have been trained to do with the expectation of an ethical and legal approach. There is the presumption that they do not need to be micromanaged. There is the assumption that there is no need to create an entire bureaucracy to oversee the business and impose fines for practices that become questionable as new medicine and new technology become available. Is the level of responsibility a doctor has for a patient much lower than the responsibility of a financial advisor to his or her client?

People who make cars determine what is needed for a car to be reliable and safe. People in management make decisions about the cost of making a car, deciding on the type of tires, brakes, steering columns, and every other piece that goes into making a car. The company chooses vendors for these products based on its standards, and it can reject suppliers if it does not think they are providing the quality that is needed. Is there a government bureaucrat overseeing all of these transactions? Does a government bureaucrat have to approve every car that gets built before it goes on the road? How many times have we seen voluntary recalls? When the company's management team realizes they have a problem, ideally, they recognize their ethical obligation and make the decision to recall the vehicle, repair or replace the part in question, and correct the problem for the future. Again, when there is a problem, the government or legal system may be called into play, but there is the presumption that the company does not need preemptive oversight into the business they know well.

Franchisors often require large investments up front from anyone interested in becoming a franchisee. People have lost their entire life's savings starting a business or purchasing a franchise. According to a recent news report, the FTC does not have responsibility to review the financials or ensure the viability of any franchising operation. There is no government bureaucracy to review the transactions between a franchisor and franchisee, and there is no oversight authority for any individual wanting to start a business. As long as the franchisee or business owner fills out the required forms and pays the required fee, anyone can start any business in a capitalist country. Can an individual make a poor decision to invest in a bad franchise, resulting in the loss of his or her life savings? Yes. Is anyone other than that individual held accountable for that investment decision? No. Why, in a free society and capitalist economy, would an individual have the freedom to invest any way he or she chooses in a franchise, but in purchasing stock in a business or group of businesses, the transaction becomes subject to scrutiny and the salesperson who sold the stock becomes liable for that decision?

As the government keeps running to the rescue, offering bailout after bailout, what is becoming more and more apparent is that there is little individual accountability expected anymore. Many people make bad decisions, and government intervention will never change personal irresponsibility. Individuals need to consistently take ownership of their own choices and accepting the consequences of mistakes, failures, and bad luck. The stock market has no guarantees. Warnings are printed on virtually every piece of marketing material, disclosing that the investment may lose value. Choosing to invest in the stock market means accepting the risk.

A faulty vehicle could mean an incompetent employee, a greedy manager, or a simple mistake. An accidental death in an operating room could be the result of doctors' lack of training, a gross error, an insurance company's greed, or a simple mistake. Though there are no guarantees in life, the United States Congress wants to give the investing public a guarantee that their investment will only go up. When it does not, the financial advisor or broker dealer must surely be to blame.

# A Tale of Two Americas

We have violated one of the main principles on which our country was founded. The United States of America represents freedom around the world, standing for justice and equality. This is the country where anyone can start with nothing and make the life he or she desires with hard work and perseverance. It seems like we are moving toward a class system and a great division. The private sector generates wealth, pays the taxes, and is held accountable for mistakes. The public sector creates nothing, generates no wealth, pays no corporate tax, and is not held accountable. It has been considered the employer for the complacent as, once hired; a person can almost never be fired.

According to Paul Lights, a professor of public service at New York University, "Very few federal employees—in the hundreds, not thousands—are ever fired on the basis of poor performance. That's out of a federal workforce of 1.86 million." He goes on to explain that the process for firing a federal employee is so cumbersome and biased in favor of protecting the employee, it becomes far too costly and time-consuming. Terminating an employee can take a year or more. Don Kettl, a professor at the University of Pennsylvania, agrees. He states that it is just too hard to fire poor performers due to a federal civil service web of antiquated rules (Holan & Angie, 2005).

According to the Cato Institute, federal employees are not fired nearly as often as they should be. In 2001, only 0.02% of non-defense industry government employees were fired. Other agencies have similar statistics. In 2001, the departments of agriculture, health and human services, and HUD each had a 0.02% termination rate. The department of education fired only one person in 2001. The department of state also fired one person, and the department of transportation fired two. Does this mean that employees in the public sector are just much better performers than those in the private sector? It would be hard to find anyone who believes that explanation. The Cato Institute provides this comment: For example, the 28,000-person State Department has fired just six employees for poor performance since 1984, yet this agency is known for its sloppiness in handing out visas and mishandling secret documents, and it even allowed Russian spies to bug a meeting room down the hall from the former secretary's office.

The dearth of federal firing is consistent with the general lack of incentives for good performance in the bureaucracy. Surveys find that most federal workers do not believe that the best qualified people are the ones receiving promotions. (Edwards & DeHavens, 2002). The report goes on to cite a study by the Office of Personnel Management, which explains that federal workers are given the message that it does not matter how you perform. As long as you continue to show up, you will automatically move up the pay scales.

Coincidentally, there have even been cases of employees who do not show up and still get paid. In August 2010, The Virginian Pilot reported a woman employed with the Community Service Board of Norfolk did not show up to work for 12 years and yet continued to get paid. The Community Services Board is an independent agency that receives funding from the city, state, and federal governments. When the reporter brought the issue to light, the agency's executive director moved forward to fire her, but what about the previous 12 years? How did an employee continue collecting a paycheck without detection for 12 years? It must be awfully difficult indeed to get fired if you can be a no-show for 12 years (Minimum, 2010).

## Conclusion

After our thorough review of the data, the following conclusions are evident. First, there is corruption in the securities industry. Second, most of the efforts being made through the legal channels and with government-mandated training have failed. Third, while laws and regulations do not stop crooks from being crooks, they do hinder good people from doing the most efficient job they can and earning the most profits a business can generate. Based on these conclusions, it is arguable that we need a new solution. In the final chaper, we recommend actions and long-term solutions to the ethical challenges prevalent in the securities industry. Some recommendations are also applicable to any private business or organizational entity.

CHAPTER **9**

# The Implications of Excessive Government Regulation of the Securities Industry

HAVING GATHERED AND tabulated the results from the survey and the interviews, we now turn to the analyses and observation drawn from the data. Observations made regarding each of the four hypotheses and further analyses of the data give clear indication of the validity of each hypothesis. The four hypotheses tested and reported in this book are presented below:

**Hypothesis 1:** Regulatory requirements and laws reduce profitability in the securities industry while failing to minimize securities fraud.

**Hypothesis 2:** Involvement of government in the securities industry is largely ineffective due to its dysfunction and corrupt practices while taxpayers continue to pay more in taxes.

**Hypothesis 3:** Education and training programs presented, and often mandated by the government, to enhance ethical behaviors in the securities industry do not work.

**Hypothesis 4:** Because fraudulent practices in the securities industry are due to a lack of commitment to do business according to the prescribed ethical practices, only human factor–based education programs can address them.

## Overall Observations

The contents of this book show that in order to address corruption in the brokerage industry, it is imperative to address the pervasive severe human factor decay in the industry and in the country to make any lasting changes and meaningful improvement.

## Government Intervention

There is a fine line between government oversight and intervention. Most respondents are concerned about too much government intervention. There is a strong indication that people do not feel comfortable with the government gaining too much control over private enterprise. However, the responses indicate the people are not ready to get rid of government oversight altogether. This is because they do not see any other alternatives. With an acknowledgement by almost all respondents that there are problems and there definitely is corruption in the industry, the respondents together want neither deregulation nor a return to the wild wild west of the early investment days. Laws implemented after the Great Depression did provide some guidelines and some protection to consumers (see Chapter 2). *The Glass-Steagall Act*, for example, was enacted in 1933, during the early days of the Depression. This law prevented certain kinds of banks from merging. When it was repealed, in 1999, it "allowed big firms to swiftly grow in size" (Gasparino, 2010, p. 31).

The Glass-Steagall Act would have prevented Citibank and Bank of America from having both banking functions and investment functions in one organization. It likely would have stopped the excessive growth of these institutions, preventing the *too big to fail* issues of 2008. Ironically, it was Citibank's CEO along with a top-ranked government administrator, Robert Rubin, Treasury Secretary under

President Clinton, who orchestrated the repeal of the Glass-Steagall regulation. The problems with the banks that became too big to fail began with the repeal of a law that had been on the books since the 1930s. The *too big to fail* banks that served as both savings and investment institutions proved that some legal restrictions are beneficial. However, with a greedy mentality and unethical approaches to business dealings and practices, the law can be circumvented or even repealed. In this case, repealing an existing law, thus allowing a high-risk activity, proved detrimental to the investing public.

When we look at how the previously existing laws have helped the industry, these respondents have mixed feelings. When we consider the occurrences of 2008, we wonder why all the compliance apparatus and regulatory requirements did not prevent the near collapse of the economy. For example, while the Glass-Steagall Act served a specific purpose and was designed to prevent exactly what happened at the large banks, Sarbanes-Oxley seemed to have no specific goal. It was largely a reflexive reaction to the accounting scandals at Enron, Tyco, WorldCom, and other companies. This round of laws, implemented in 2002, placed an undue burden on small firms, created many additional and expensive administrative requirements, and caused more intrusion into the operational procedures of the firm as well as the privacy of the client. It resulted in much more paperwork being mailed to clients, at great cost to the firm and with questionable results. After all the adjustments, with the entire industry made to accommodate this law, how did it help anyone? Most people are still unsure of its primary purpose. Investment clients today receive many required mailings of privacy rights and annual updates just to appease the federal regulators. Clients complain about the extra paperwork. Firms hate the expense and the time it takes to do the massive mailings. No one seems to understand what this is accomplishing.

## Legal Response

Regardless of historical failures, the government continues adding more laws such as the newest *Dodd/Frank law*. They try to look responsive, and yet many Americans know it is just a game. Dan Walsh, in Case Study 1D, explains it this way:

Before the government drafts new laws they really need to look at how it will impact all of us and what kind of effect it will have in the future. They are too shortsighted. They are just out getting a lot of press. Politicians are interested in looking good but they are not worried about coming up with something that works.

Has the legal response solved the problem? As our respondents in the survey indicate, there is a need for someone to oversee the unethical components in the industry; however, the current solution involving government and legislation is not the favorable choice. Survey statement number 12: The less involved the government is in the business, the better. While 44% of the respondents agreed with this statement, 35% disagree. The interviewees make similar comments. Frank Laden provides commentary on the needs for compliance and regulatory oversight:

It is necessary because there are some people you can't trust in this business. They make it hard for the rest of us. If you don't have compliance, there is no credibility for brokers in general. Customers feel more comfortable knowing compliance is looking out for them. It helps people feel more comfortable with the industry in general. The customers need to know there are consequences for those that do bad things in the industry. They need to know there is justice. It's like having a speed limit. Not everyone follows it, but there is a way to punish those who don't.

Abe Hall also agrees there is the need for some type of oversight: "You have to have rules and guidelines in the securities business. There is too much opportunity for abuse otherwise. Just like regulations they have to be enforced consistently. They serve as a deterrent for bad behavior and establish expectations for the firm's employees and advisors." Barring a better solution, government regulation, it seems, is a necessary evil. It is better than having no system at all guiding behaviors and, as Frank Laden clearly explains, a consequence or instrument for appealing for justice.

## Politicization of the Process

From the data, it is clear that because there are bad people in the industry, there is the need for some method of controlling behaviors or eliminating participants bent on unethical practices. The data also reveal that there is a low level of expectation that the government or the legal system is the best place to look for answers. Though government presence in the securities industry may be better than its absence, the real challenge is in knowing what the net benefits are. The apparatus the government creates to respond to any problem or manage anything tends to be excessively expensive and far less efficient than solutions applied in the private sector. The costs continue to grow as government expands in response to each crisis in private industry. The size of the bureaucracy grows and expenses increase.

What are the benefits? We can look at our recent history. If the government oversight apparatus was effective, how did we end up with failures such as the accounting scandals of Enron, the explosion of the dot.com industry, the failures of major Wall Street banks, and the near implosion of the economy in 2008? How do we explain Madoff? How do we explain AIG and Lehman Brothers? Based on the collected empirical evidence, it is undeniable that the oversight apparatus has failed and, regardless of additional laws, increased expense, and continued hand wringing, government will never be the answer.

When politicians get involved, it is certain that they have a greater desire to pursue their own interests than be concerned with bringing improvements to the industry. Congress makes laws that create problems such as requiring banks to give loans to those without the creditworthiness requirements to qualify for a loan. Once the inevitable happens, those same individuals in Congress seem completely shocked when the scenario that bankers warned them against, massive defaults on loans, occurs. People who did not have the credit and the income to qualify for a loan soon defaulted on those loans, setting up a chain of events that was predicted by many and ignored by all who mattered. The root of this disaster can be traced back to the United States Congress, the same people grandstanding and pointing the finger of blame at Wall Street. One example of the hypocrisy is the Community Reinvestment Act. This was backed by many in Congress. This act, along with others, forced banks to lend to poor communities for housing. These were many of the bad loans packaged into subprime housing bonds. These loans naturally went into default, as expected. Congress initiated what became a domino effect of financial disaster, and yet not one of them accepted responsibility. Rather, they exonerated themselves of any culpability while holding hearings to embarrass everyone else (Gasparino, 2010, p. 151).

Politicians have another reality that appears primary in their motivation. That is the need to get re-elected. With this in mind, money flowing into their campaign funds is at the top of their priority list. Where is there a guaranteed revenue stream directly into Washington, D.C.? It is Wall Street, of course. In the 2008 election, in the middle of the economic crisis, a substantial amount of Wall Street money went to the Obama/Biden campaign. Typically, Wall Street hedges its bets, giving money to both sides of the aisle in an effort to have control regardless of which party is in power. Consequently, neither party has clean hands, but we focus on the most recent election because the influence is clear given the current economic situation.

According to Charles Gasparino's book, *Bought and Paid For*, as some of the most prominent figures on Wall Street invested huge amounts of money in the Obama campaign, they became very involved with decision-making once he was elected. The speculation was that these Wall Street figures invested so heavily and so early that they ensured this unknown, inexperienced politician would gain enough exposure at the outset of the campaign to topple more seasoned and higher-profile candidates. Why did Wall Street choose Obama, a liberal Democrat not particularly friendly to business? According to Gasparino, they felt that he could be bought and controlled, whereas John McCain, the Republican candidate, was known for being an independent and a maverick, not someone to be controlled. As Wall Street is imploding, a safer bet is someone who can be bought and consequently indebted rather than a senior senator and military officer with a long history of strong positions. Senator John McCain, Senator Hillary Clinton, and others were already well known to Americans and could get elected without as much indebtedness to Wall Street.

With Wall Street kings and queens sitting cozy in the White House, how will decisions be made regarding the future of the securities and banking industries? One can surmise changes would be largely favorable to the major players while continuing to increase burdens on those small firms without the president's ear and the front line participants with no political power, financial advisors. From the public's perspective, it looked like the government is coming to the rescue. The very large firms have inside people at the White House to influence policy, so it is not too challenging for them, while they can also have their extensive legal teams back in New York researching the path around any potential new legislation. "Wall Street's friends are placed throughout the Obama cabinet, thus ensuring that Wall Street has had a huge say in the reshaping of the financial business. CEOs like Dimon and Blankfein had made numerous trips to the White House attempting to ensure that the President doesn't do anything that really costs them any money." (Gasparino, 2010, p. 56)

While the big firms influence the law, small firms just wait for the impact and pray for survival. Responses to the survey indicate an awareness of all of these practices. The majority of respondents are clear that the current system is not satisfactory and that the federal regulation is not the solution. The confusion comes in trying to figure out the options. People are aware that there is a problem with corruption and there is a sense that something needs to be done, but most do not have an alternative.

## Profitability and Productivity

Most respondents recognize that there is a loss of profitability tied to the current process. Financial advisors are changing how they do business and adapting their processes for regulators, not for their clients. Any industry that is regulated has the same components. As a result, some of the non-industry respondents were probably reacting to these issues in their own industry.

Anyone who works in a position of authority and understands the involvement of government oversight is aware of the impact on and expenses involved with compliance. Though for large companies compliance is a nuisance, for smaller companies the requirements to satisfy compliance can mean the difference between remaining in business and being profitable or having to give up and shut down the company. For small companies, it can obstruct virtually all areas of business as the few employees available must deal with the compliance needs and regulatory demands. Even if a company has a perfect track record and has never had any complaints or issues, it is entirely at the discretion of the auditor how much time to spend reviewing any company. Another statement from the survey: "Efforts made to comply with regulatory measures increase the cost of doing business." This statement addresses how regulatory costs impact business and 81% agreed that it does impact profitability.

They also responded similarly to another statement, agreeing that resources channeled into compliance activities lead to reductions in productivity. Nearly everyone surveyed believes that the costs associated with complying with regulations are significant enough to impact business. Interestingly, while 89% say that complying with regulatory measures increases the cost of doing business, they also believe that they are guided by their own moral compass. If they are guided by their own moral compass, what is the justification of the costs associated with complying with legal and regulatory measures? Also, 74%

stated that most financial advisors are honest people. Consequently, if people follow their own moral compass and most people in the industry are deemed trustworthy, why would the government insist on spending taxpayer dollars for regulation that 89% of the respondents believe increases the costs of doing business?

Increased costs are naturally passed on to the consumer. Investors, therefore, pay more for investment advice from professional advisors so that unlicensed and inexperienced non-financial bureaucrats can review the work of the professional, licensed, and experienced financial expert. The reduction of productivity also means that there is less time available for financial advisors to do their job. Time spent on non-productive, non-service–oriented activities reduce the amount of time financial advisors can spend helping their clients: reviewing their accounts, paying attention to changes, and looking for improved investing opportunities. They are too busy doing paperwork for the various government and non-governmental entities.

## Paperwork and Pencil Pushing

The individuals interviewed for the case studies all touch on the expense and time invested in activities unrelated to client service. The paperwork is overwhelming. Case Study A, Al First, talked about all of the paperwork, data entry, and *back office* activities that consumed much of his time. In Case Study B, Ben Pool provides an example of the process for completing an application for an annuity. In Case Study 1E, Ed Warsaw describes the excess paperwork as well.

According to Ed Warsaw in Case Study 1E, the increase in paperwork over the years has made clients less responsible for their own decisions. "As clients are faced with a mountain of overwhelming forms all written in legalese, most people just give up attempting to read and understand the forms and, instead, just trust their broker and sign the forms where he or she tells them to." This has the exact opposite effect of what was intended. The purpose of all the extra required forms and disclosures are to provide more information to the consumer. Instead, it ends up providing less, as they are so overwhelmed, they do not read what they are expected to read. This actually makes it easier for an unethical broker to practice unlawful activities. A client who does not read the forms can be signing things with a complete lack of awareness. This is one example where the government's intrusion and resulting regulatory involvement actually makes it easier to complete a variety of unethical activities. As Abe Hall states, "We are in a service business. We are dealing with people who for the most part are financially illiterate, which creates a huge opportunity for abuse."

## The Cost of Doing Business

Most financial advisors are honest people. While 76% of the respondents agree with this statement, it is interesting to note that the money spent to oversee financial advisors continues to grow year after year. Additionally, 74% of the respondents state that they believe most brokers are honest people. If most brokers are trustworthy and try to do the best for their clients, why is so much time and money spent on training, educating, investigating, pursuing, and prosecuting brokers? Could it be that just a very small number of individuals are employed in the unethical business practices that have brought the American economy to its knees? If so, what is the answer?

Most of the American public has become convinced that government intervention is not the solution to problems of unethical business practices. People know that government regulation hardly ever works. People are aware that it costs money, which affects the bottom line of the firm, reduces profits, and adds costs to the consumer. According to Abe Hall in Case Study 2-A,

> The single biggest obstacle to profitability is the cost of compliance. The increasing compliance requirements are forcing the securities industry into a "bigger is better" mentality, and that is not good for the small investor, who the larger wire houses do not want to serve. In other words, you have to be big in order to afford the increased costs associated with

increased regulation. This puts pressure on the smaller firms to either grow organically in a hurry or combine with a larger firm in order to survive. Broker dealers must continuously update their technology and add staff to handle the increasing regulatory demands.

As a manager in a small broker/dealer, Abe Hall had to make budgetary decisions resulting in additional resources going to the regulatory and compliance area of the firm. As the overhead in this area grew, net income for the firm diminished. Profits were squeezed and resources stretched. As small broker/dealers become less profitable, many begin closing their doors. In 2008, as the recession caused a reduction in income while the cost of compliance continued growing, many small to medium broker/dealers made the difficult decision to close or merge with a larger firm. This ultimately costs the consumer, as less competition results in fewer choices.

## Regulator Responsibility and Ability

A total of 51% of the respondents agreed with the statement: "Most government regulators do not understand the securities industry." This is a fairly disturbing result, because many of the respondents are industry people. They come in contact with regulators from FINRA, the SEC, and various state authorities fairly often. They have a good idea of what regulators are looking for, what they are chasing down, and how they handle investigations and audits. For 51% of them to believe that these regulators do not understand the business is concerning. Only 18% disagree with that statement, which is certainly stunning. The balance of the respondents neither agrees nor disagrees. This is due to a lack of knowledge. It is worth repeating that 51% of respondents believe that most government regulators do not understand the securities industry. How is it possible for people who do not even understand the industry to be charged with overseeing and maintaining the integrity of the system? This provides one significant piece of the puzzle. Regulators cannot be effective if they lack the knowledge and skills necessary to do the job. They are being asked to do what may be impossible.

In addition to the survey responses, concerns are expressed by those interviewed about the knowledge and capabilities of the current regulatory bodies such as FINRA and the SEC. Ed Warsaw provides an example of how good intentions can exacerbate a problem rather than solve it when those charged with making the corrections understand the actual problem:

> They are talking about fiduciary standards. It sounds nice, but every investor right now probably thinks we already have a fiduciary standard. Can't we just leave it alone? They need to define it and understand what it even means. They want to make it a criminal act to not do what is in the best interest of the client. How does anyone know what that is for certain? For example, people pay to have their accounts managed right now. They pay three to four times as much for investment advice as someone in an XYZ fund account paying upfront charges and the small 12b1 fees (commission overrides). The 12b1 fees (commission overrides) are only 25 basis points (for this company). That is all the customer pays ongoing for years of service and any time the advisor spends with them. Yet the regulators want to eliminate 12b1 fees. The problem that they discovered is that some clients are paying 12b1 fees, yet they are not assigned to an advisor. The answer is to assign them to an advisor, not eliminate the fees for everyone else who does have an advisor. Whether the account is managed or not, some reps spend more time than others but many of them do spend time, they do the right thing, and they earn that fee. Some clients never hear from their advisors, but eliminating the fees is not the right answer.

In the example provided by Ed Warsaw, it is clear that, while the regulatory community has good intentions, they are mistaken in their application. They are correct that it is unfair for investors to pay fees for service they are not getting. Yet most financial advisors who do the right thing spend a great deal of time with their clients with little or no compensation. The minimal compensation in 12b-1 does not even come close to the value of the time and energy that a good financial advisor will spend with his or her client over the course of many years. Though some clients are extremely demanding regardless of the size of the fee, financial advisors continue to serve their needs. Elimination of the 12b-1 fees would actually transform a minor problem into a huge one. If financial advisors do not receive any compensation at all, there is no incentive to maintain clients. This move will actually encourage financial advisors to write new business, earning the large up-front commission and then refusing to provide any ongoing service because there is absolutely no incentive to do so. While there is no financial incentive to keep the account, there is a deterrent to keeping the account, namely liability and service. Investors will find themselves getting fired by their financial advisors.

The other issue that Warsaw raises is that of fiduciary standards. This is another example of how regulations are dictated to the financial advisor community without any real understanding of how they are to be implemented. In this case, a violation of the law can now be considered a criminal act. Given that many in the financial advisor community have expressed complete confusion, who is willing to risk their career and their freedom with a mistake? Some financial advisors have simply retired or left the industry rather than continue this battle to understand laws that make no practical sense to those on the front lines of the business yet can cost them greatly. The liability has become greater while the rewards are getting smaller. Frank Laden is a very successful financial advisor with many years of experience, a large client base, and a continual high level of income. His perspective on the increased risk is explained as follows: "If I didn't make the money I make, I wouldn't put up with the risk. I try to do the right thing for the client and it's a win/win. My philosophy is that if I do what's right for the people, I will make money, but I can't get clients just to make money. If I wasn't making so much, though, this amount of work, stress, and risk would not be worth it."

So, as the government looks for ways to minimize the reward of the work by reducing profit while increasing the risk, good financial advisors are more likely to leave the industry while unethical brokers will continue to find ways around the laws. Arguably, this is the operation of Gresham's Law in the brokerage industry. That is, the creation, implementation, and enforcement of bad laws in the brokerage industry increases the number of unethical brokers, and by so doing, chases out the more ethical brokers and advisors. Some financial advisors walk away from the business in frustration, tired of spending so much time on paperwork and so little time earning income, and others are chased out of the business by frivolous claims. Finally, some just realize there are much easier and less stressful ways to earn a living.

## Taxpayer Impact

When financial advisors cannot get any clear direction on the application of a law, which happens often, they try to do the best they can and work with their compliance team for interpretation. The compliance officer will do the best job he or she can to understand and interpret the law as provided. If the compliance officer approves of a transaction, the financial advisor feels confident that he or she is making a good decision. The financial advisor follows the process. The compliance officer gives the input that he or she believes to be accurate. It is then decided to move forward with the transaction. In spite of these checks and balances, problems can still occur. If, at some future date, a new rule is written or an old rule is changed or a different interpretation is given, a transaction that happened years prior can be considered suspect. It is like getting a ticket for failing to stop at a stoplight in 2008 when the stoplight was installed in 2010. The securities industry works in such a way that it can review old business with new eyes and see things differently. Everyone may have very good intentions, but the result becomes convoluted.

Financial advisors and compliance managers are forced continuously to be aware of pitfalls and landmines as they protect their firms and themselves from anything and everything. Some well-meaning, well-intentioned, and ethical financial advisors do lose their careers from one mistake. Carl True, who at the time of this research, was experiencing a claim against him, describes it this way:

> The goal of compliance is to make sure brokers do the right thing for clients, but as it is now all they are doing is practicing defensive advising because compliance is only looking out for liability and any long-term repercussions rather than the best interest of the clients. Specific products become a hot button in the industry, and then they become something bad after the products have been available for years. Products are available, and then all of a sudden they are bad. They need to give clear guidelines and tell you if something is wrong instead of coming back after the fact. The goal should be prevention and they should be proactive on product, not determining later that it is not a good product.

Carl True was facing a complaint from a client at the time we contacted and interviewed him to provide some insights regarding these issues for this book. He discussed the process and his experience further through a face-to-face interview in the following manner:

**Researcher**: What do you think the biggest challenge is to profitability in the brokerage industry and what do you think needs to be changed in order to make the industry more profitable?

**CT:** Having to be so concerned about liability in the future. I know advisors who are staying away from any 1035 exchanges or anything that is just not worth the risk even if it's a good investment for their client. Annuities are a great product with the guarantees and other bells and whistles, but it's not worth it to the representative to do one. Even with those who have older annuities where there is no surrender charge, it would be good to put them in a new one with all the new things,—guaranteed death benefit, and others—but advisors won't do it now because of all the paperwork required and the liability exposure.

**Researcher**: Overall, are you satisfied with the way government regulators oversee the business? If not, what would you change?

**CT**: No. In this system I have to prove I'm innocent. Allegations are a dark cloud and just the allegations can shatter your career overnight. Business is affected and the renewals of my license can be affected. They can put whatever they want on the website for everyone to see. Even before any determination is made, it's a public humiliation.

**Researcher**: What is the worst thing (i.e.: unethical, illegal) you have seen in your years in the industry?

**CT**: My current situation. I feel violated. It's a dark cloud over everything. I have anxiety wondering what to tell my current employer. I have to explain it to people. Even to get my insurance license renewed I had to report that this complaint was going on. If my license doesn't get renewed then I'm done. I can't earn a living. As a representative the responsibility is to the client, not to the children. The children just are greedy and want the money. The complaint states that I abused my client and they called me a crook and a scum bag. They accused me of elder abuse. They are trying to say their mother was elderly and didn't know what she was doing. That's not true. She was a wonderful lady and she was my friend. We stayed friends a year after I stopped being a financial advisor, met for lunch once a month. She continued to call for advice and even asked my opinion when her daughter called wanting money.

During the arbitration, Carl True was vindicated. Unfortunately, the allegation alone impacted him and remained a cloud over him for over a year.

Dan Walsh explains his view: "Politicians get involved and end up hindering our ability to do our job. We shouldn't be so encumbered. Too many rules make it so difficult to conduct business and you just can't do it anymore. Because it's so convoluted and difficult, it's not helpful."

There seems to be a complete toss-up on the benefit that new government laws have provided to the consumer. Survey Statement: "Regulatory decisions and additional laws made in Congress have benefited the securities industry and the consumer." With approximately 30% saying laws have benefited the consumer, 30% stating that they have not, and 30% not sure, that is a very unconvincing argument for additional laws to be passed, such as the Dodd-Frank reform of 2010.

The respondents in this study are uncertain existing laws are beneficial, and there is no clear support for more laws if history is any indicator. Statement 19: The government should add new laws and provide more oversight in the securities industry. A total of 63% of the respondents disagree with that statement. A total of 15% of respondents agree with the statement, indicating their desire to have government continue to be involved in the securities industry. The remaining 19% neither agree nor disagree. If existing laws have not provided more protection for the consumer, what is the benefit of the additional cost?

Another survey statement: "Government should not be involved in the provision of regulatory oversight in the securities industry." While 66% of respondents agree that most brokers are trustworthy and try hard to do the right thing for their clients, there is reluctance to agree that the government should completely be uninvolved with the regulation of the industry. The data reveal that the respondents think there must be some oversight and they believe that there are unethical aspects of business practices in the industry. They also express that government will not be the best choice to address issues of business ethics. Given the option to make a choice between no oversight or government oversight, they prefer to have government oversight. However, if there was an alternative, perhaps the support for a government solution would be minimal. There are numerous examples of business crisis or scandals that the regulators missed. Can we really expect those individuals tasked with regulatory oversight to foresee ethical violations or judgmental lapses? Does it make sense to place the heavy burden of regulatory micromanagement over the many in order to prevent the few from perpetuating illegal and unethical activity? How much success can we even expect for our investment of time and money in the regulatory apparatus?

Maintaining the regulatory apparatus and extensive governmental bureaucracy is very costly to the taxpayer. Many regulators try very hard to be responsible, yet have a difficult time keeping up with the industry. It requires a great deal of experience and the SEC continues to have high turnover, resulting in a lack of seasoned professionals. In his book *Bought and Paid For*, Gasparino states:

> Many government officials I have come across during my career make easy targets for investment bankers. They are largely unaware of these dangers because they're political appointees and, as a result aren't schooled enough in high finance to really know what they're buying. Their main goal is to keep government functioning—even in its often dysfunctional state.

There are many reasons government is not the solution to private-sector problems. Even with all the best intentions, it is a difficult, if not an impossible task. While the taxpayers spend an ever-growing amount of money on the increasing bureaucracy of regulators over-seeing the business, the results are questionable.

We can draw a conclusion from a collection of statements viewed together. Survey statement: "Most of the brokers I come in contact with are people I trust." A total of 56% of people say they trust the brokers they come in contact with. A corresponding survey statement: "Most financial advisors are honest people." A total of 74% of respondents agree with that statement. Yet when we provide the following statement, it is very revealing: "I trust government officials and want them to oversee the securities business." A total of 12% of respondents agree with that statement. To the statement: "I trust the government to do things well," only 7% agree with that statement. Consequently, while 74% of respondents think financial advisors are honest, only 12% trust the government to oversee the brokers and only 7% trust the government to do anything well. While only 7% think government is competent and trustworthy, this is the group expected to oversee a group that is evaluated as honest by 74% of respondents.

The question then becomes, why have we established one group of people to oversee another group of people. Does this even make sense? Those hired to oversee the industry are paid with taxpayer dollars or industry-mandatory contributions. Financial Advisors and brokers are compensated through their own innovation and sales skills. Most are paid only when they complete a transaction and earn a commission. If they do not sell, they do not get paid. If they do not work, they do not get paid. If they are unsuccessful at their job, their income will reflect it. The population of people hired to oversee them, however, are compensated at the same rate no matter how often they work or what they accomplish. Even if they fail miserably, as many would contend they had in failing to foresee the many bank and brokerage failures of 2007-2008, their compensation remains the same. Regardless of the dismal history of failures in the financial industry, this group of people has increased their ranks, grown its bureaucracy and, worst of all, increased its salaries.

Survey respondents show that they understand the confusion, and this is reflected in their answers. Yes, they think financial advisors should be held accountable, but they also understand that problems in investing at the retail level can be a poor decision made by an investor, greedy management, or any number of things. Individuals are skeptical of financial advisors as they are skeptical of any other groups of people, but the results of the survey were very clear that most brokers do a good job. There are a few bad brokers, just like there are some bad individuals in any group. Respondents also agreed in large part with the statement that greedy management can also be to blame for problems in the brokerage industry. Does the same scenario exist in other industries? According to Art Row,

> The government is, for the most part, dysfunctional. Unions protect substandard workers; the outreach programs to "disadvantaged" people vice hiring the best qualified has significantly lowered the performance expectation. Unionized government workers have little or no incentive to perform efficiently. The more inefficient they are, the more people they need, and therefore the union ranks expand and the unions gain more power.

It does not matter what the industry is. Government intervention, regardless of all good intentions, tends to make a problem worse. As Art Row describes above, efforts at outreach programs to disadvantaged workers essentially now create another kind of disadvantaged worker, one who cannot compete fairly because of all the protections the government provides its select groups at any given time. Unionized public-sector workers are notoriously less efficient, less motivated, and yet higher paid. As we learn more and more about the increases in the compensation and benefits of public-sector workers, particularly the exceptionally generous retirement programs, it becomes apparent that we have successfully created a monster. This monster is insatiable and unsustainable. The public-sector employees have become the Achilles heel of government at all levels.

# CHAPTER 10

# Dealing with the Moral Challenges in the Securities Industry: The Significance of the Human Factor Model

EACH OF THE four hypotheses has been proven true through the survey and case studies, which have been reported in previous chapters. Because those in charge of the systems are unable to deal with severe human factor decay, they have been unable to solve problems in the securities industry. This being our reality in the United States, it is time to look for other solutions. Adjibolosoo (2012, pp. 103-104) defines severe human factor decay as follows:

> Severe human factor decay is a syndrome evident in a person's expression of lifestyle choices that are reflective of negative personality traits. It trumps the personal desire for virtuousness and promotes a lifestyle rooted in bad attitudes, behaviors, and actions. Severe human factor decay is the primary root cause of the human condition. Any act of social injustice is a perfect replica of the images of severe human factor decay...Severe human factor decay is a natural outflow

of negative human factor. It is a serious hindrance to the establishment of harmony and peace. It is a staunch enemy to productivity growth. Its austerity paralyzes the engine—positive human factor—that makes the social institutions function and remain functional over time. It stalls the wheels of the vehicles of family, government, schools, economy, law, and religion. It initiates and propels the uses and abuses of technological progress. It is the sole factor that lies at the heart of the practice of identity theft, sexual harassment, spousal/child abuse, and corruption in its diverse forms in any communities. Severe human factor decay damages the lives of citizens and denies them the ability to attain their human potential and sustain higher productivity levels. It renders these people unproductive. Their attitudes and behavioral practices are more destructive than constructive.

The four areas addressed are the implications on the excessive involvement of government officials for the profitability of brokerage firms, taxpayers, the net benefit of government training programs, and the ethical and moral challenges being faced in the industry. With the analysis of the four areas of inquiry, a great deal is learned. The four hypotheses, each corresponding to one of the foregoing areas of interest, include:

**Hypothesis 1:** Regulatory requirements and laws reduce profitability in the securities industry while failing to minimize securities fraud.

**Hypothesis 2:** Involvement of government in the securities industry is largely ineffective due to its dysfunction while taxpayers continue to pay more in taxes.

**Hypothesis 3:** Education and training programs are presented and often mandated by the government to enhance ethical behaviors in the security industry.

**Hypothesis 4:** Because fraudulent practices in the securities industry are due to a lack of commitment to do business according to the prescribed ethical codes, only human factor–based education programs can address them.

In what follows, we present the conclusions drawn from the data collection process and analysis. These conclusions are used as the basis for the recommendation we make in this book for public policy.

## Observations

The securities industry has been infiltrated by unethical people who engage in immoral practices. Just after World War I, the growth of the securities business exploded, increasing the demand for brokers, as most of the population became investors. During this time, the industry needed to relax the hiring qualifications for brokers in order to increase the supply of capable, licensed staff to place orders and handle investment transactions. As those with questionable qualifications and dubious motivations entered the marketplace, the reality of the deterioration of ethical practices in the securities business emerged and escalated.

Various government leaders and other public servants tried to intervene after the stock market crashed in 1929. Unfortunately, they did not address the underlying cause of the problem: severe human factor decay. Legal remedies have been too weak to prevent unethical brokers and other industry participants who navigated around them. Training programs did not address ethical issues because they concentrate solely on the development of human capital, which is only one of the six components of the human factor. The wholistic development of the six components of the human factor is required for a healthy labor force performance in the diverse marketplaces. While those individuals intent on finding unethical methods through which to increase their own wealth continue to find avenues, hard-working and honest financial advisors find the barriers to business becoming more and more time-consuming and frustrating.

## Training and Human Capital

No matter how much training, bankrupted of the six dimensions of the human factor, the taxpayers finance, it will never be enough. The government-mandated training modules concentrate solely on human capital acquisition. This training program concentrates on encouraging brokers to hone the quality of their human capital, yet the development of human capital alone is not enough. It accomplishes one out of the six components of the human factor. As presented in Chapter 2, the human factor is composed of spiritual capital, moral capital, aesthetic capital, human capital, human abilities, and the human potential. Essentially, then, our government and the public education system develop people who are bankrupted in all the other dimensions of the human factor. Yet, undeniably, without having honed the other components of a person's human factor, he or she is bereft of the real opportunity for enhanced productivity and joy in life. Arguably, the exclusive emphasis on the development of human capital alone guarantees a population of greedy and self-absorbed narcissists.

The other five components of the human factor are neglected. While we continue to pour more money into one area of human factor development, the rest continue to decay. In the securities industry, it is obvious to most that the financial crisis did not stem from a lack of human capital in those countries that have been severely impacted. The United States, for example, is probably the nation that has the most highly educated brains in the whole world. Some of the best financial and economic minds in the country work on Wall Street. There is an extensive wealth of human capital on Wall Street, and all that the country's best colleges have to offer are residents of New York City. Many on Wall Street are proud graduates of the best business schools, such as Harvard, Cornell, Penn State, Stanford, UCLA, Yale, MIT, and Northwestern. Undeniably, though, the largest financial crisis in history happened under the watch of these academically brilliant people at the peak of their careers. The crisis did not occur because people were not academically educated enough. The crisis occurred because people are bankrupt of the other key dimensions of the human factor. Without having developed these other dimensions of the human factor, leaders in diverse professions will not commit themselves to morally based lifestyle choices (Adjibolosoo, 2005). While we may continue to develop human capital at a rapid rate, we are creating a society of single-dimensional people who are poor in the other invaluable aspects of the human factor.

Regardless of the efforts that many political, government, and industry leaders have made, the problems of unethical practices in the industry remain, and costs continue to increase. As the kinds of unethical practices that prevailed in the 1920s still exist in 2012, it is obvious that the problem has not been minimized. Involving the government and applying legal solutions to ethical lapses has not worked. In addition to the questionable benefit of government involvement in the securities industry, the excessive financial expense of maintaining oversight has become its own negative impact on the severity of problems in the brokerage industry.

Those suffering from severe human factor decay have other motivations for knowledge. They might benefit from information, knowledge, or training as it provides a more defined road map for fraud and unethical activity. Some may not have unethical intent, but they will not benefit from training programs. They will just do the required amount of training mandated by the government. It will not benefit them as they do not care, are not approaching it with a positive attitude, and may even be resentful of the Big Brother interference in their lives.

The primary argument of this book is that when we spend the money intended for oversight and regulatory compliance on human factor–based education at all levels of academic training and leadership development, we will minimize acts of fraudulent business practices and subsequently increase company profitability in the industry. The need for such regulatory involvement will be reduced as more people become inner-directed, as the connection between heart and mind is developed in the direction of principle-centeredness. As the need for regulatory involvement is reduced, less taxpayer money needs to be spent on the oversight bureaucracy. Brokers are able to pursue more profitable activities rather than being inundated with paperwork and hoop jumping.

Those who fail to develop a healthy human factor must have their credentials revoked and licenses withdrawn, thus removing opportunities for abuse in the industry. As the regulatory burden is minimized, the cost and time-consuming activities associated with appeasing regulators will be reduced. Profits will increase, and more firms will have the ability to compete fairly. Small firms will no longer be forced out of the market because their owners commit to do business ethically. Consumers will have more choices. Competition will increase service. Perhaps most importantly, we will reduce the risk of the *too big to fail* companies having the size and strength to pull down the entire world economy, as we saw in 2008.

Problems in the securities industry, including fraud and irresponsible and unethical behavior, will never be corrected by adding laws, new regulations, and additional regulatory bodies. More bureaucracy and additional oversight will not correct the real problem of severe human factor decay.

## The Human Factor

> Arguably, the problem of *severe human factor decay* cannot be improved with the enactment of additional laws.

Human factor–based education must include programs to help participants to hone the six components of the human factor. As noted earlier, these components include spiritual capital, moral capital, aesthetic capital, human capital, human abilities, and the human potential (Adjibolosoo, 2005, p. 45). According to Adjibolosoo, in order to develop quality leaders in business as well as government, every leader must possess and also commit to express qualities such as love, joy, peace, patience, kindness, goodness, faithfulness, gentleness, and self-control (Adjibolosoo, 2005, p. 44). In the securities industry, if brokers, management, and all involved staff members are steeped in the positive qualities of the human factor, most unethical business practices will cease to exist or will be minimized. It requires the kind of training that goes far beyond increasing skills—investing in increased human capital but including all six areas of the human factor as well.

There are people in the securities business today who are guided by the positive qualities of the human factor. They are kind and patient, helping clients with their needs. They are gentle and thoughtful, listening to the stories and hopes and dreams of those they serve. They experience peace and joy in just the simple act of talking to people, and they appreciate the gift of being able to help people reach their lifelong goals. There is intrinsic motivation and value in working with clients and their families through the good days and the bad. These are the kinds of people we must have in the securities industry. Unfortunately, though, these are also the people being chased out by overregulation and random persecution. Those who spend every day working hard and helping people regardless of the amount of profits attached are people who must be encouraged to stay in the business and rewarded for the value they bring. Instead, they live in a world where they are treated as criminals by the regulators and, if any investigation or complaint arises, they are guilty until proven innocent and the burden of proof is completely upon them. Any random accusation can result in a loss of income or even an entire loss of career. Even a mistake or a consequence that no one could have possibly predicted can become a deadly cross to bear for any independent broker.

What brought us to this point? In many other industries, government historically has been uninvolved. In the early years of the investment industry boom in the 1920s, the government was uninvolved in the securities industry. When the stock market crashed in 1929 and the country went into depression, people from all walks of life debated the issue and, based on the outcome of an election, the message was clear. The investing public wanted some protection and asked the government to play referee. Government leaders accepted this assignment, determined a lot of answers, and developed an entire bureaucracy to appease the public. Sadly, they did not solve the fundamental cause of the problem—severe human factor decay.

While there were some fraudulent and unethical business activities at that time, there was also simply, in the words of Kenneth Galbraith, *irrational exuberance*. This was the responsibility of the investors. They had planned for only positive returns. While fraud and unethical behavior were problems, greed and unrealistic expectations also played a role. Blaming the broker became the norm, and self-responsibility was not addressed. This reality was our experience since then till today—and definitely hereafter regardless—of which player was in the game. Be it investor, broker, or management, the evidence of severe human factor decay has been and continues to be overwhelming.

It is imperative that we begin as a nation to address the problems of severe human factor decay in the industry and in the country to make any lasting changes and meaningful improvement. We are forcing businesses into bankruptcy and individual brokers into retirement. We will continue to see fraudulent and unethical activity in the securities market. We will continue to drain the public coffers as we chase after solutions that will never work.

## Benefits of Human Factor–Based Educational Training

With a human factor–based educational training program, we will minimize the ethical failures and, consequently, the need for Congress to pass new laws and create additional rules and oversight authorities. With the decline of oversight comes a corresponding reduction in expenses. As we start to chip away at the huge bureaucracy, securities firms benefit as well as the taxpayers. As individuals become educated in enhancing the positive qualities of the healthy human factor, they will make decisions with internal motivation and they will develop internal controls. The thought process that drives those to unethical behaviors will change. The greed and desire for power will be minimized, as will those activities that result in ruin for investors and the general public.

If people are really guided by their own moral compass, then why do we still have so much fraud and unethical activity? Perhaps the compass is not set properly. If we reset the moral compass to accurately provide principle-centered direction, that internal compass that resides in each of us can really do the job it is intended to do. As the rust and ruin upon the compass causes decay inside the human spirit, the arms of the compass point people to the wrong directions. Once the decay is dealt with and the face is no longer encrusted with the damage of dilapidation, we can begin with a fresh approach to human factor and leadership development.

While it has not been clearly identified as a human factor issue, pieces of the real problem have been identified since the first securities crisis in 1929. When President Roosevelt attempted to find ways to protect the consumer from future problems on Wall Street, he addressed a lack of education. He identified a need for education for those tasked with the responsibility of handling the investments of the public. As mentioned in Chapter 2, Roosevelt commented on education in terms of integrity: "I do not mean a college diploma, but the inability to understand the country of the public or their obligation to their fellow men" (Parrish, 1970, p. 109). President Roosevelt understood that it was not just about knowledge or skills, but about an awareness of their obligation to others, the responsibility to do the right thing for the client.

Roosevelt continued to comment on the needs of the industry in terms of human factor development when he identified honesty as a missing piece: "Such legislation should give impetus to honest dealing participants in the industry and thereby bring back public confidence" (Parrish, 1970, p. 47). Roosevelt knew that the industry participants needed more than just human capital. In terms of the human factor, he was addressing the need for spiritual and moral capital.

Throughout the years of the debate, the discussion often results in some minor attempt to address the human factor. Most often, it is referred to as business ethics. Some leaders recognize missing components as part of the problem. Many are too challenged by their own human factor decay to accurately identify and solve problems in the country, in the business sector, or in the securities industry. Failing to find a complete solution is why it is never solved. New laws are band-aids that stop the initial bleed each time a new wound develops. Sadly, though, they ultimately fail to deal effectively with the primary source of the problems on hand—severe human factor decay.

## A Tale of Two Employees

Over the years, we have developed a dual system of employment in this country. We have the private sector and the public sector. At one time, the public sector was considered the less desirable but more secure option. In the past, public-sector employees made less money, had fewer opportunities for advancement, and did not have the rewards that private-sector employees had. The trade-off was that the public sector virtually guaranteed continual employment regardless of performance. It was considered a safe haven even for the unmotivated and uninspired employees. The private sector was the higher-risk option. Merit-based pay was the norm. Expectations were high. Terminations happened frequently and performance mattered. The private sector expects productivity and self-responsibility. There are consequences for poor performance and even mistakes. The trade-off was higher pay and the opportunity to earn bonuses, raises, and perks.

Today the roles have reversed. Public-sector employees now, in many cases, make more money than private-sector employees for the same job. Public-sector employees have generous retirement benefits and pensions that have not been part of the private sector since the 1970s, when companies like IBM, Xerox, and Kodak led the way into dramatic reorganization of employment agreements in order to secure a sustainable future for the business. As private-sector employees began paying more and more of their own retirements and health care, public-sector employees were given more taxpayer-funded retirement income and fewer years of work to earn it. Private-sector employees put money into their own 401k for retirement, while public-sector employees have taxpayer-funded retirements. Private-sector employees have been steadily paying more of their health care while public-sector employees largely pay little or none. Private-sector employees are working more years to be able to afford to retire, while public-sector employees have successfully negotiated such generous packages through their unions that it is not unusual for them to retire as early as 55 years old with a fully vested retirement program. The functional expectations in the two types of employment arrangements, however, have not changed. Public-sector employees are virtually guaranteed a job as long as they choose and can almost be assured that regardless of performance they will not be fired. Private-sector employees have become the scapegoat of any company squeezing the bottom line. Private-sector employees have lost jobs in unprecedented numbers since 2007, and those who remain employed often have gone with little or no raise for years. With profits down, private employers cannot pay employees more, even if they would like to. With tax revenue down, public employees continue to enjoy the annual raises their union contract guarantees, resulting in the deficits most states and many cities are grappling with today.

Concerns about this system have been mounting, and warnings have been issued for years. The free ride is coming in to the station, but many are unwilling to accept that reality. During the economic downturn in the years of 2008-2011, investments have slowed as people are cautious about putting more money into the stock market. Many securities firms have closed their doors, and financial advisors have retired and changed careers in response to the slowing demand of the business. We should be seeing a corresponding reduction in employment in the agencies tasked with oversight of the securities business. Yet there is no report showing a significant decrease in payrolls of any of the major government entities charged with this responsibility.

As more public sector workers are unionized and fewer workers are dependent upon their own ingenuity and hard work, a malaise has set in. It is very disheartening to work in an environment where those who work hard are rewarded no more than those who barely work. As workers become more demoralized, they become less connected to their own human spirit. They become more robotic and less self-aware. Union employees in public-sector jobs are a nameless, faceless bunch. As a result of collective bargaining, they become a part of a bargaining unit, not an individual. The destruction of the individuality and the sense of self-responsibility continue to erode the human factor.

Private-sector employees, on the other hand, may be earning less in salary than they anticipated when they chose their careers. Financial advisors spent many years educating themselves for the industry with the expectation of a fairly lucrative living and pleasant retirement. The role reversal with the public sector has left many of them questioning their career choice. Financial advisors have a great deal of risk. People in the securities industry and private business in general are treated as individuals with the upside and the downside. A failure to perform can result in termination. One customer complaint can result in termination or even banishment from the industry. Reduction in profits often results in layoffs. Pensions are almost non-existent in private-sector companies. Quality people in the private sector are almost compelled to start looking at the public sector because it may be the best option in terms of security with guaranteed salaries and pensions and health care for life. This role reversal may result in some of the best and brightest who once were recruited to Wall Street instead going to work in the post office.

## Entitlements and Investments

Galbraith refers to the continued interest in new products rising to popularity in the securities industry as an erroneous belief on the part of so many individuals in this country that "effortless enrichment is an entitlement." In Chapter 2, we discussed the growth of entitlements and the entitlement mentality. This is part of the human factor decay. More people expect to be taken care of rather than earning their own way in the world. There is greed in many corners of this country, and some spend their days coveting their neighbor's goods while refusing to do the necessary work to achieve a higher level of earning, not to mention greater self-satisfaction.

According to Galbraith, *euphoria* is based on getting without merit and withdrawing without ever depositing into the system. When President John Kennedy told us to ask ourselves what we could do for our country, people felt a call to action and a mission to a cause greater than oneself. In the 21$^{st}$ century, there seems to be a rejection of hard work and a desire for easy money. This attitude stems from a decaying human factor and results in a resentful society and a bitter community of people. This attitude also results in outlandish expectations that cannot ever be met. Individual investors want to enjoy the benefits when the stock market rises but they refuse to be held accountable when the stock market goes down. Brokers get blamed. Individuals do not accept responsibility for their own choices. The securities industry does not cause all of the world's ills. The world is ill, and we need to look to ourselves for improved health, not government regulations.

Have we solved the problem? Perpetrators find new products that have not yet been regulated and new loopholes that have not yet been exploited. Does anyone think additional laws will prevent a new product from coming onto the market with the same high-risk strategies that have been brought to the market in the past with so much profit readily available? Not a chance. The only solution is to change the paradigm entirely. In each sector of society, we need to implement a human factor–based training and leadership program. The securities industry has many players, and no one is completely blameless. Regulators, bureaucrats, congressmen and women, financial advisors, managers, marketers, and compliance staff all suffer from the same malady: the severe human factor decay.

## Making the Necessary Repairs

The best place to begin is the beginning. In general terms, that means making our schools into human factor–education academies. We can no longer secularize our schools and expect godless beings to turn into moral adults. To begin, we need to start with the basics of our education system and work into the social/economic structures of business and government, including compensation, incentives, and oversight. The goal for each area is to generate the energy and character of a positive human factor.

## Human Factor-Based Education

The American labor force must possess certain characteristics. This is the primary reason why a long-term solution to the problems in the securities industry requires dramatic improvement of our education system. A human factor–based education program builds critical competencies and moral and spiritual principles. Students would be taught to develop their talents and focus on their abilities in their education. Parents obviously play the most critical role in teaching and modeling to their children ethical behavior; however, if schools become an environment where ethics are praised, the value of integrity is addressed openly, and the likely outcome will be a generation of students with a healthy human factor.

The change in the education system would make a tremendous impact on the health of the nation in the long term. We need to move away from dependency on the public-sector school systems and allow parents more choices in education. With charter schools and free market involvement in education, students will no longer be at the mercy of whatever public instruction bureaucrats deem to be important. The impact of human factor–based education will result in more complete individuals. Children will grow into adults who are capable, competent, and moral. They will exhibit excellent moral character through their judgments, decisions, and treatment of others. They will show kindness, compassion, and awareness of issues and individuals beyond their own needs. They will develop their minds while developing their spirits and moral sense. They will invest in their own potential and concern themselves with their role in the world. Students will learn to think for themselves and make ethical decisions, and they eventually will join the workforce as positive contributors in all areas of the human factor, beyond simply human capital.

# CHAPTER 11

# Observations and Recommendations for Public Policy

WE CAN KEEP adding more legislation, but we just perpetuate the cycle severe human factor decay and moral practices at diverse marketplaces. Unethical people on Wall Street, just like bad people anywhere, find ways to defraud the public, thus enriching themselves. When the big banks asked for a bailout, the government stepped in with taxpayer dollars. The bank executives learned that they can continue to take risks because there is no losing position for them. With high-risk practices, if they win, they make obscene amounts of money, but if they lose, the government bails them out and they still make obscene amounts of money. They do not need to monitor their behavior or balance the risk, because the downside is covered by the American taxpayers. The risky practices continue. We add new regulations, which result in additional oversight, meaning additional employees, additional agencies, and nongovernmental organizations.

Whether it is finding a previously unregulated product, creating a process that successfully avoids oversight, or any other approach to circumventing the system, where there's a will, there's a way. Those who were victimized demand action. Congress adopts laws, government agencies implement them, and, in order for companies to comply, more employees have to be hired. Additional regulatory authorities are needed to implement the laws, public sector workers are hired, and the second, silent victimization happens. Taxpayers get another huge bill. A bigger bureaucracy means additional oversight authorities, increased expenses for broker/dealers, and higher costs to the clients. More public-sector workers generally results in more union power and higher costs for taxpayers, and the cycle continues.

The unemployment rate remains high in this country, and more companies are refusing to hire employees with all of the economic uncertainty. In the securities industry, many companies no longer exist post-recession. Those jobs will never come back. Brokerage firms that continue to compete are doing so with less. Some are outsourcing jobs to India and hoping the cost savings will allow them to survive. The securities industry is one of the most regulated industries in existence. This is why the financial sector of the economy continues to struggle to get back on its feet. In addition to the lost revenues experienced due to the recession, the industry continues to be challenged to keep up with the ever-growing burden of laws and regulations. Many laws can also be applied in relation to the size of the company, taking into consideration the ability for smaller companies to comply and yet stay competitive.

An improved human factor would allow the securities industry to grow and be more profitable. With fewer ethical violations and a healthy human factor, the burden on taxpayers would be reduced. Growth in this industry would provide employment opportunities for many people. This industry particularly hires recent college graduates with finance and business degrees. We continue to see many graduates in this country jobless or underemployed due to the economy and because white-collar jobs are heading to India and elsewhere. Reducing the regulatory burden and providing an environment in which business can thrive and afford to hire will reduce the unemployment rate in this country. We need our young people to feel motivated and encouraged as they enter the workforce, not frustrated with the lack of opportunity.

# Leadership

What is the motivation for candidates to run for office or for anyone to accept a leadership role? According to Adjibolosoo, there are three reasons—power, wealth, and recognition: "Most politicians rise to power as a result of one of these motivations or a combination of them with their leadership skills" (Adjibolosoo, 2005, p. 44). The severe decay of the human factor does not stop at the securities industry or in the corporate world. The government agencies and regulatory bodies charged with oversight all have plenty of their own problems and corruption can be found in the public sector as well as the private sector. The government regulators charged with overseeing the securities industry have not done a perfect job. Those in Congress making the laws often have their own agenda, and even the president has had some questionable motives in dealings with Wall Street.

Severe human factor decay is evident in politics and throughout our government. We all are aware of the excessive money, questionable campaign practices, impact of lobbyists, and unions. The use of earmarks for pet projects and the influence Congress members can exert through this process has naturally corrupted the system. It certainly seems that the motivation to get re-elected far surpasses any other priority, and decisions are made in that context.

When we begin implementing human factor–based education, eventually people will be drawn to politics for the right reasons. Their motivation will be to serve and to improve the country, not just for their own self-glorification. While there are some people currently doing a great service to their country and their constituents, there are many who have long since lost sight of the mission and the purpose, and they have lost touch with reality. Lured and hypnotized by the exotic power of Washington, many have been lost to the abyss of narcissism. They see themselves as a higher order of individual than those lowly masses they manage. These people cannot possibly be effective, but a new generation of leaders can take office and begin steering the ship. "When one accepts any leadership role, it is important to have the right principles and the positive human factor" (Adjibolosoo, 2005, p. 129).

Adjibolosoo notes further that those in leadership must have clarity of mind and be fully committed to the mission: "They may need to accept consequences for making a principled choice. This is the role of a leader" (Adjibolosoo, 2005, p. 129).

> Leaders are expected to work hard to perfect their craft. They should spend time training, honing their skills, and becoming better leaders in order to do the best job they can for the people they serve. They should protect the weak, curtail the bullies, and defend freedom and justice whenever and wherever possible. They cannot be fearful or weak. They must think of others before themselves and see the opportunity to serve as a gift. These individuals are prepared to pay the ultimate price for the pursuit of principle-centeredness in mission accomplishments. For any leaders to be effective, it is also important to identify the issues that need to be considered as the leader enters the leadership role. It is impossible for a leader to be successful without knowing what the issues are and how to go about dealing with them (Adjibolosoo, 2005, p. 129).

We need the kind of leaders described by Adjibolosoo. With a healthy human factor, guided by principles, leaders in the securities industry can set new standards and begin the process for self-governing. We will have better leaders or leaders better prepared to lead. Leaders in business and government can change the way the country functions, which will spur the economic growth needed to ensure that America remains the beacon of hope and light of democracy for generations to come.

There are many historical and existing failures of leadership evident in the United States. A thin layer of superficial attractiveness covered the decay for many years. When the financial crisis occurred in 2008, the toxic waste that has been fermenting erupted and rose to the surface, bringing a stench that wafted around the world. While many warned about it, no one took leadership to prevent it.

The larger perspective, beyond the securities industry, includes all businesses. Private-sector businesses have to produce more, sell more, and work harder to pay higher taxes to support the growing public sector. As public sector unions demand higher wages, more benefits and greater pensions, the private sector staggers under the weight. The government entities tasked with paying the respective contracts for teachers and various other public workers are going bankrupt. Current services are being restricted, reduced, and eliminated, all in the effort to keep up with the benefits and pension payments of government employees and retirees. This is a financially unsustainable system. Our leadership has failed us.

Many unionized government employees are, generally, unmotivated and it is not their fault. They are lulled into a state of apathy as union bosses control their lives and manage their careers. They are not incentivized and are almost never fired, and they continue to get salary increases annually, regardless of quantity or quality of work. They receive very generous benefits and pensions for as long as they live. They do not ever have to increase their workload or level of responsibility to obtain raises, and they will not be rewarded if they perform to exceptional levels. This is what unions create. Those who are intrinsically motivated usually become quickly disillusioned, not to mention overloaded with work, as they make up for their lazy counterparts. It is almost hazardous to your health to be a hard-working, capable employee when you are surrounded by those who are not.

The securities industry exemplifies a microcosm of our nation's failures. The securities industry has some fraud. It has some business-people participating in unethical behavior just as it is the practice in every other industry. It also has hard-working, dedicated participants who are well-intentioned. The securities industry has been burdened with multiple levels of government and nongovernmental bureaucracies that exist solely for the purpose of overseeing individual industry players and ensuring they do their job properly. As mentioned previously, whether this process is even possible is questionable given the complicated nature of the business. For a 20-something-year-old recent college graduate to review the investment decisions of a 60-year-old financial advisor with more than 30 years of experience seems ridiculous. Does the entire bureaucracy as a whole catch some things? Yes. Is it even reasonable to expect them to catch everything? No. Many regulators are capable and do a good job. They believe they are protecting the investing public, and they want to see justice in the system. The motivations of many are commendable. The reality is that even if the regulators were all highly experienced, exceptionally intelligent, and provided with all the resources imaginable, it would be impossible to expect them to detect every single source of fraud in any industry. As long as we continue to live with severe human factor decay, we will always see those bent on corrupting the system for their own gain.

Americans have become comfortable and complacent, considering our lives to be very safe, secure, and relatively easy. Even the "poor" in this country are actually rich by standards in other countries. America is still a wealthy nation, and we have resources, foundations, and an educated and motivated citizenry. Most Americans want to be employed. They want to be productive, and we are appalled at those of our citizens and community members demanding the free ride. We are frustrated with those who are greedy, materialistic, image-conscious, and lazy. With gradual improvements in the quality of the human factor, we will begin to see improvements in society, business, and, specifically, the securities industry. We can anticipate a decrease in crime, reduction of debt, and minimization of unplanned pregnancies and drug dependencies. We could anticipate an increase in loyalty, hard work, and family values. America will be back on track.

While the securities industry has been maligned by the media, and the blame for the economy is largely aimed at Wall Street, this is a distraction from the real problems. Wall Street contains greed just as Washington contains greed. Wall Street contains hard-working Americans just as Washington contains hard-working Americans. Wall Street is experiencing severe human factor decay just as Washington is experiencing severe human factor decay. To pay Washington to oversee Wall Street is largely futile and costly. The general public, referred to as "Main Street," are also not the unsuspecting victims our leaders in Washington, D.C. would have us believe. Main Street is certainly not lined with angels. Those who took large loans and accepted irresponsible levels of debt must be held accountable also. No loan officer held a gun to the heads of those taking the mortgages that they could not possibly afford. Individual irresponsibility certainly played a role in our recent crisis and, until corrected, will likely play a role in future challenges.

Until we begin to correct the problem of severe human factor decay in this country, there is no area of industry, economy, or community that will grow. Each individual must take responsibility for his or her own integrity. Once we address this issue and invest the time and energy to implement the solution, we can be back on the way to the kind of economic prosperity that Americans are driven to pursue. Our nation was born under the banner of life, liberty, and the pursuit of happiness. Economic prosperity is the foundation that provides the freedom for those individuals and communal pursuits.

# Bibliography

Ackerman, Ruthie, 2010, How Will New Rules Impact Family Offices, Bank Investment Consultant, 3/15/2010, retrieved from www.bankinvestmentconsultant.com.

Ackerman, Ruthie, 2010, Goodbye 12b-1 Fees? Bank Investment Consultant, 7/21/2010, retrieved from www.bankinvestmentconsultant.com.

Adjibolosoo, S. 2011. *The Human Factor Foundation of Free Market Efficiency.* New Delhi, India: New Century Publications.

Adjibolosoo, S. 2005. *The Human Factor in Leadership Effectiveness.* Tate Publishing, Mustang, OK.

Adler, Joe, 2010, Did Dodd-Frank Resolve the Too Big to Fail Issue or Give it New Life? American Banker, 12/23/2010, retrieved from www.bankinvestmentconsultant.com.

Apuzzo, Matt, 2010, Ad Impact: Government bank auditors got big bonuses, San Diego Union Tribune, 3/18/2010, retrieved from http://signonsandiego.printthis.clickability.com.

Apuzzo, Matt, 2010, As meltdown loomed, regulators got bonuses, San Diego Union Tribune, 3/19/2011, p. A3.

Associated Press, 2011, Auditor: Financial Overhaul Law Costs $1Billion a Year, Moneynews, 3/29/2011, retrieved from www.moneynews.com/

Barney, Lee, 2010, Pitt Gives Dodd-Frank Bill an F, Bank Investment Consultant Magazine,12/6/2010, retrieved from www.bankinvestmentconsultant.com.

Barrett, Larry, 2011, Regulatory Confusion Keep Advisors, Broker-Dealers In Limbo, Bank Investment Consultant Magazine, 3/7/2011, retrieved from bankinvestmentconsultant.com.

Byrne, John, No Excuses for Enron's Board, Business Week 7/29/02, p. 50-51

Cheney, Richard and Cheney, Lynne, 1983 Kings of the Hill, Touchstone, division of Simon and Schuster, New York, NY.

De Bedts, Ralph, 1964, The New Deal's SEC: The Formative Years Columbia University Press, New York, copyright 1964

DeGregorio, William A., 2002, The Complete Book of US Presidents, Random House, New York, NY.

Edson, Richard, 2011, Federal Agencies: We need more Staff, Fox News Online, Retrieved from foxnews.com. 9/30/2010

Edwards, Chris, &DeHavens, Tad, 11/02, The Cato Institute Bulletin, The Tax and Budget Bulletin, retrieved from catoinstitute.com

Fromson, B.D., The Last Days of Drexel Burnham, Fortune Magazine, May 21, 1990, p. 90-96

Galbraith, John Kenneth, *A Short History of Financial Euphoria,* Penguin Books, New York, New York, 1990

Gasparino, Charles, 2010, Bought and Paid For, *The Unholy Alliance Between Obama and Wall Street,* Sentinel Publishers, member of Penguin Group, New York, NY.

Gasparino, Charles, 2007, *King of the Club,* HarperCollins Publishers, New York, NY.

Graziano, Anthony M., and Raulin, Michael L. *Research Methods, A Process of Inquiry*, Harper Collins Publishers, New York, NY, 1989

Gingrich, Newt, 2011, 1,986 Reasons to Repeal, Human Events Newsletter, 1/19/2011, retrieved from humanevents.com.

Holan, Angie Drobnic, 9/15/2007, Firing Federal Workers is Difficult, Politifact.com Magazine, retrieved from Politifact.com.

Jamieson, Dan, 2011, SEC Should step up scrutiny of FINRA: A Study of the SEC's internal operations suggests that the agency needs to pay closer attention to the SRO, Investment News, March 11, 2011, retrieved from investmentnews.com.

Kaper, Stacy and Ackerman, Ruthie, 2010, GOP Pledges Major Changes to Dodd-Frank, Fannie and Freddie, CFPB, American Banker, 11/4/2010, retrieved from Americanbanker.com.

Kass, John, 2011, Billy Daley as Obama's chief of staff? I love it, love it, love it, The Chicago Tribune, 1/5/2011, retrieved from www. chicagotribune.com.

Mehta, Nina, Thomasson, Lynn, and Barrett, Paul, 2010, The Machines that Ate the Market, Bloomberg Businessweek, 4/26/2010, retrieved from www.businessweek.com.

Menchaca, Paul, 2010, FINRA's Ketchum emphasizes Fiduciary Standard: Increased Scrutiny of Variable Annuities

Meyers, Jim, 2011, Outrage: Freddie and Fannie Execs Pocketed $35 Million In Taxpayer Money, Newsmax, 4/1/2011, retrieved from newsmax.com.

Miller, Richard I. & Pushkoff, Paul H. 2002, Regulations Under the Sarbanes-Oxley Act, Journal of Accountancy page 33-36.

Minimum, Harry, 8/26/2010, A no-show for 12 years, worker in Norfolk still paid, Pilot Online, retrieved from http://hampton-roads.com/2010/08/noshow-12-years-worker-norfolk-still-paid.

Mitchell, Donna, 2009, Compliance Officer Role Gains Importance, Bank Investment Consultant Magazine, 5/19/2009, retrieved from bankconsultantmagazine.com.

Mitchell, Donna, 2011, Who Is Really Going to Watch Small Firms? Bank Investment Consultant Magazine, 2/22/2011, retrieved from bankconsultantmagazine.com.

Monks, Matt and Davis, Paul, 2010, Bank CEOs Offer More Clarity on their Revenue Conundrums, 9/15/2010, retrieved from www. bankinvestmentconsultant.com.

Morris, Dick and McGann, Eileen, *Fleeced,* Harper Collins, New York, NY, 2008

Parrish, Michael, E., *Securities Regulation and the New Deal*, Yale University Publications, New Haven, CT, 1970

Phillips, Susan and Zecher, Richard, J., 1981, The SEC and the Public Interest, The MIT Press, Cambridge, Massachusetts and London, England.

Prial, Dunstan, 2010, Obama Repeals SEC FOIA Exemption, Fox Business Report, 10/5/2010, retrieved from www.foxbusiness. com/markets.

Randall, Maya Jackson, 2011, Head of Crisis-Panel Says Warning Signs Weren't Heeded, The Wall Street Journal, 1/27/2011, retrieved from wsj.com.

Rove, Karl, 2011, Obamacare Rewards Friends, Punishes Enemies, The Wall Street Journal, 1/6/2011, retrieved from wsj.com.

Snyder, Bill, 2011, Hackers find new way to cheat on Wall Street – to everyone's peril, InfoWorld, 1/6/2011, retrieved from infoworld.com.

Sobel, Robert, *The Great Bull Market, Wall Street in the 1920s.* WW Norton and Company, New York, Copyright, 1968.

Sproull, Natalie L., 1988, *Handbook of Research Methods: a guide for practitioners and students in the social sciences.* Scarecrow Press, NY and London.

Staffwriter, 2011, NCUA Workers Skirt Federal Pay Freeze, Credit Union Journal Daily Briefing, 1/4/2011, retrieved from cujournal.com.

Staffwriter, 2010, NCUA Jacks up Spending for New Round of Examiner hires, Credit Union Journal Daily Briefing, 11/18/2010, retrieved from www.cujounnal.com.

Staffwriter, 2010, NCUA Missed Red Flags on Big Failures, Credit Union Daily Briefing, 11/3/2010, retrieved from www.cujournal.com.

Staff Writer, 2010, NCUA Examiners Asleep At the Switch In U.S. Central Failure,

Stephens, Warren A., 2010, The Financial Reform Proposals on the Table Won't work. So What Will? A Banking CEO Has Some Ideas. Fortune Magazine, 4/12/2010, p. 48.

Stock, Howard, J., 2010, Bank Executives Doubt Frank-Dodd's Effectiveness, Financial Planning Magazine, 2010.

Stock, Howard, J., and Mitchell, Donna, 2010, almost All Investors Support a Fiduciary Standard, Bank Investment Consultant, 9/15/2010, retrieved from www.bankinvestmentconsultant.com.

Stock, Howard, J., 2010, FINRA Proposes All-Public Arbitration Panels, Bank Investment Consultant, 9/28/2010 retrieved from www.bankinvestmentconsultant.com.

Story, Louise, 2010, A Secretive Banking Elite Rules Trading in Derivatives, New York Times, 12/11/2010, retrieved from www.nytimes.com.

Story, Louise, 2010, Lehman Channeled Risks Through 'Alter Ego' Firm, New York Times, 4/12/2010, retrieved from www.nytimes.com.

Wall Street Journal. (Eastern edition). New York, N.Y.: Sep 2, 2010. pg. C.20

Wisconsin, State of, 4/27/2010, Quantitative and Qualitative Data Collection Methods, retrieved from http://people.uwec.edu/piercech/researchmethods/data 9/5/2010)

www.ingramcontent.com/pod-product-compliance
Lightning Source LLC
Chambersburg PA
CBHW020304290526
45784CB00003B/1355